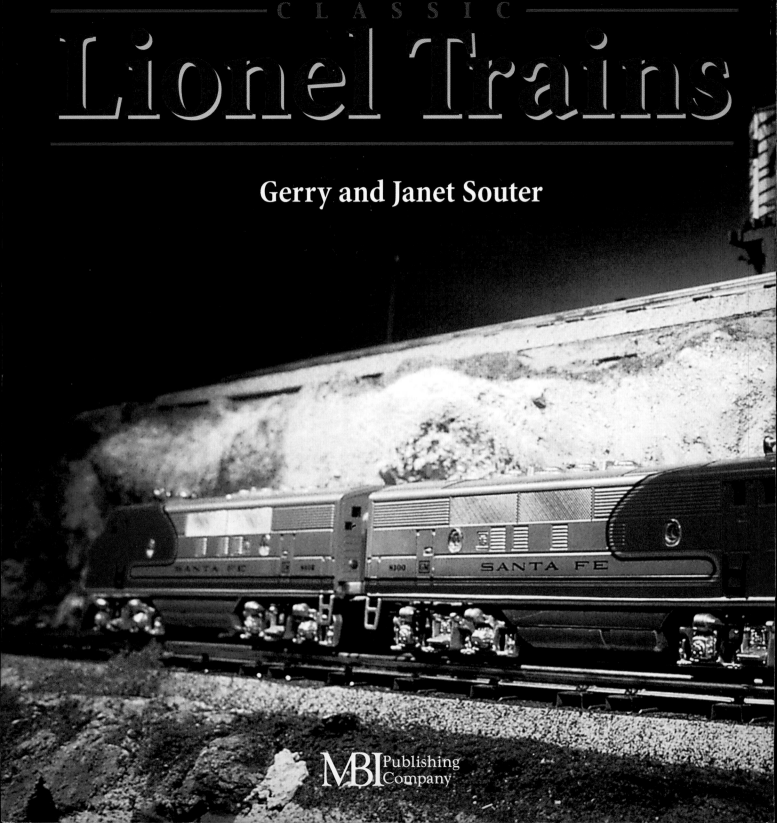

CLASSIC

Lionel Trains

Gerry and Janet Souter

MBI Publishing Company

Dedication

To Mitch Kuhn, fellow train nut, and Debbie Hayes of the Carail Museum.
Their efforts made the photos possible and the hard work fun.

First published in 2002 by MBI Publishing Company, Galtier Plaza, Suite 200, 380 Jackson Street, St. Paul, MN 55101-3885 USA

© Gerry & Janet Souter, 2002

All rights reserved. With the exception of quoting brief passages for the purposes of review, no part of this publication may be reproduced without prior written permission from the Publisher.

The information in this book is true and complete to the best of our knowledge. All recommendations are made without any guarantee on the part of the author or Publisher, who also disclaim any liability incurred in connection with the use of this data or specific details.

We recognize that some words, model names and designations, for example, mentioned herein are the property of the trademark holder. We use them for identification purposes only. This is not an official publication.

MBI Publishing Company books are also available at discounts in bulk quantity for industrial or sales-promotional use. For details write to Special Sales Manager at Motorbooks International Wholesalers & Distributors, Galtier Plaza, Suite 200, 380 Jackson Street, St. Paul, MN 55101-3885 USA.

Library of Congress Cataloging-in-Publication Data
ISBN 0-7603-1138-2

Edited by Dennis Pernu
Designed by Kou Lor
Printed in China

Front cover: Lionel's F3 came along in 1948, opening a whole new product line—namely locomotives modeled after diesel-electric prototypes, in this case one from GM's Electro-Motive Division. Joshua Lionel Cowen was not shy in voicing his dislike of diesel power. In fact, the Lionel F3's initial 10,000-unit production run went ahead only after it was agreed that the company would produce a New York Central version as well as a Santa Fe, and that the two railroads would help defray the cost to produce the expensive dies.

Frontispiece: In the 1950s, Lionel's full-color ads pushed sight *and* sound. Lionel used rail sounds narrated by the famous radio sportscaster Bill Stern.

Title Page: Over the years, the F3 was continually modified—much to the delight of today's collectors. First issued in O gauge only, it was later adapted to run on O27. Numerous liveries were also added. However, those sporting the Santa Fe's famous "war bonnet" livery easily remain the most recognizable Lionel products.

Back cover:
Even the rivet counters were impressed in 1937 when Lionel unveiled the 700EW, whose prototype was the popular 4-6-4 Hudson. Here, a 700EW motors over a trestle with *Rail Chief* passenger cars in tow. Lionel went so far as to come within three rivets of a real scale model!

Rolled out in 1953, the colorful, well-proportioned, and beautifully executed Model 6464 boxcars became the most popular and most prolific pieces of rolling stock Lionel ever made. Over their lifetime, they were produced with 29 number designations and a variety of subtle differences.

Contents

Acknowledgments

The following people offered their trains, time, and expertise to this project. Without their help, there would be no book.

Richard Kughn and his Carail Museum, Detroit, Michigan
Susan Childers, curator, Carail Museum
Chris Rohlfing
Harry Dode
Steve Esposito

Top
A 1930s Lionel catalog shows "famous" engineers who recommended Lionel trains for their own kids and grandchildren.

Left
The December 1931 issue of *Popular Mechanics* shows Bob Butterworth with his grandson and the 400E.

Introduction

In 1969, Lionel toy trains were little more than crates of parts in a warehouse and a few shaggy sets gathering dust on inventory sell-off shelves. The last employee out the door had turned off the lights. The company crashed after almost 70 years of beating off every challenge, crushing every competitor, and slip-sliding through nets of legal and financial peril. The boss was dead, his children had fled with their stock options, and cold-eyed moneymen were leeching off what could be salvaged from the tattered Lionel logo. This book examines the rags-to-riches-to-rags saga of Lionel from 1900 to the late 1960s.

The American toy train evolved from cast-iron and wood pull-toys to sophisticated electric playthings at the end of the nineteenth century. Depending on which continent you're standing on, the question of who came up with the first electric toy train can be debated. The name Lionel arrived on the scene in the United States just as the country was emerging as a world power following the 1898 war in Cuba. That event thrust the United States onto the world stage, and the country's national ambition and energy were on display. Invention and new ideas filled the air—from the new gas buggies beginning to putt along American

A dual-motored 402 electric rumbles past a well-dressed young man and his dog. Standard Gauge was called the "Rich Kid's Gauge."

ROAR OF THE 20TH CENTURY

No other model railroad trains in the world are so true to actual details as Lionel. You want realism, don't you? That's what you get in Lionel!

Let us send you the new Lionel Railroad Planning Book and catalog. It is a beautiful book for any boy to have. Contains 46 pages of full color pictures, with description details. Get it and show it to "DAD" and mother. They will help you select your Lionel set for Christmas.

If you have a Lionel Model Electric Railroad get the Lionel catalog and pick out some new accessories to make your set more complete. But be sure to send for the Lionel catalog today! The Lionel Corporation, Dept. A, 15-17-19 East 26th Street, New York, N. Y.

FREE! New Lionel Railroad Planning Book and Catalog in Full Color

Lionel Electric Railroads Are Priced from $7.00 to $325.00

LIONEL
ELECTRIC TRAINS
MODEL RAILROAD ACCESSORIES ♦ "MULTIVOLT" TRANSFORMERS
The Lionel Corporation, Dept. A, 15-17-19 East 26th Street, New York City

A pre-stock-market crash ad in *American Boy* shows the "Roar of the 20th Century" in the form of big, expensive Standard Gauge trains.

streets and roads lit by electric lights to vast industrial empires just gaining steam. Toys grew from simple playthings to teaching tools, helping to show children their future roles in this ambitious society. Girls got dolls and tea sets; boys got trains and soldiers. So much for role models.

More than 100 years later, the name Lionel is still listed among American toy makers. Despite its apparent doom at the end of the 1960s, it has become one of the most recognizable icons of the twentieth century and continues on into the twenty-first. Lionel's successes, blunders, experiments, collapses, rebirths, and eventual survival make an incredible story that should be a case study in every university business course.

That story began in the last couple of months of 1900, as 23-year-old inventor Joshua Lionel Cohen searched for a sales gimmick to sell his little electric motor.

Cohen was a born entrepreneur with a gift for mechanical tinkering. He was short, dark, and balding and came from a prosperous, middle-class family that set a respectable kosher table. Back in 1900, when Cohen was a restless young man searching for his fortune in the cavernous hodge-podge of New York City, patents were dealt like playing cards. The nineteenth-century world had been left behind in a flurry of inventions; anything electric led the charge into the future. Cohen had invented a doorbell, battery-detonated fuses for naval mines, a photographic flash powder igniter, a flashlight, and a small fan. The fuses earned enough cash to develop new ideas, one of which was the battery-powered fan motor. The fan was a dud, but the little motor had possibilities.

The legend of Joshua Lionel Cohen strolling down a Manhattan street, stopping to look into a toy store window, and visualizing a little battery-powered train circling a track to attract attention to the display has been told ad nauseum. In a stroke, he had conceived the killer product that would make his fortune. Cohen seized the moment and realized his future: Cohen would be a window dresser!

Well, it didn't work out that way. For $4, the toy store sold his little cheese-box gondola that ran on strip-steel track. Then another was sold. And another. Soon, Cohen and his partner, Harold Grant, couldn't build the little trains fast enough. The cheese box that was never designed to be a toy became one, and Cohen's dreams of becoming the first electrical window dresser were dashed. He became a railroad baron instead. Thousands of miles of Lionel track would be laid in his lifetime. So what if his railroad empire stretched across living room rugs?

Once Cohen entered the toy business, he focused on what needed to be done. There were a lot of electric trains around. Most were from long-established German manufacturers such as Märklin

JUST look at this wonderful Lionel Outfit—with its "Twin-Motor" locomotive! Think of the fun of running a real railroad of your own with this big "Twin-Motor" locomotive that pulls twenty cars. The amazing thing is that a Lionel outfit with "Twin-Motor" locomotive costs no more than outfits of like size with single motor locomotives of other makes. (There are ten types of powerful Lionel single motor locomotives in addition to the "Twin-Motor.")

Your Dad will be right with you on Christmas morning. He'll agree with you that only Lionel trains are good enough. He'll understand the superiority of Lionel one-piece all-steel car and locomotive body construction and the hand-enameled and baked finish of all Lionel trains—just like automobile finishes.

Lionel train outfits and accessories can be run from any electric light socket with a Lionel "Multivolt" Transformer—or from dry or storage batteries.

Demand Lionel Trains at your dealers—Be sure of satisfaction. There's a Lionel Outfit priced to fit every purse.

Be sure to send post card for the handsome Lionel 40-page catalog printed in four colors.

THE LIONEL CORPORATION   52-C EAST 21st STREET
NEW YORK CITY

LIONEL ELECTRIC TOY TRAINS
&Multivolt Transformers

Father and son bond with Lionel trains in this late-1920s *Popular Mechanics* ad. Notice that the unusually complex rug railroad layout takes up most of the floor.

and Bing. They offered not only wind-up and electric trains, but clever accessories as well. Quality-conscious middle- and upper-class Americans who purchased toys for their children knew it was both penny-wise and chic to "buy German." In America, the firm Carlisle & Finch had been making toy trains and trolleys since 1896. Ives had been making cast-iron toys and trains since the 1860s, offering wind-up locomotives that

looked like their prototypes pounding down America's high iron—the fastest man-made creations of the time. Cohen needed more than a battery-powered cheese box.

With his electric gondolas going out the door as quickly as the new Lionel Manufacturing Company could build them, Cohen came up with the idea first for an electric trolley and then for an electric locomotive based on a Baltimore & Ohio prototype (also electrically powered) that moved trains through tunnels surrounding Baltimore. By 1910, Lionel's patented Standard Gauge three-rail track presented a challenge to the competition, as did a nifty little steam engine powered by a "transformer" rather than expensive dry-cell batteries or incredibly dangerous sulfuric acid wet cells.

By then, Cohen had two children of his own, given to him by his vivacious wife, the former Cecelia Liberman. Also, due to the odious whiff of anti-Semitism that wafted through the largely Protestant toy-industry corridors, he Americanized his last name from Cohen to "Cowen." Though he must have agonized over the decision, Cowen never once denied his heritage and remained an important part of the Jewish community. With that aside, Cowen loaded up on his competition and exploded into the marketplace.

An almost endless stream of wonderful toys began to flow from the fertile imaginations and clever observations of Lionel's creative staff. Cowen was the whip hand, the guiding force, and the final decision-maker. His philosophy can be put in a nutshell by using the fictitious but oft-quoted *Model Railroader Rule Book*:

Rule Number 1: It's my railroad.
Rule Number 2: If there's anything you don't like on the railroad, see rule number 1.

That is the essence of this story: Lionel's roller-coaster ride from that first powered cheese box in 1900 to virtual domination of the industry from the mid-1930s to the late 1950s. From that pinnacle of success, Lionel descended to what appeared to be an ignominious end in 1969. The story is a case history that could give an MBA student goosebumps.

A 1937 scale model 700EW Hudson in the Lionel catalog hauls its articulated tin *Red Chief* passenger train.

The tale is told in detail and with journalistic candor in our book, *Lionel: America's Favorite Toy Trains* (MBI Publishing Company, 2000). In this volume, we concentrate on the model trains themselves—they help tell the story of each era.

At this point, we must also define our meaning of the word "classic" as it relates to Lionel. Unlike the real trains featured in other MBI Enthusiast Color Series books, Lionel produced thousands of each toy train. A large investment went not only into the manufacturing process, but also into marketing and distribution. In all other aspects, toy trains paralleled the trends of the real railroads. As newer, faster electric and steam and diesel locomotives were produced, toy train manufacturers kept pace via their own miniaturized designs.

When steam was replaced by diesel motive power, models of Electro-Motive, Alco, and Fairbanks-Morse locomotives appeared on toy train layouts. In the late 1950s and early 1960s, as jet aircraft stole passengers and Interstate highways

allowed trucks to absorb the long-haul freight business, the railroads began a steady decline. The toy train marketplace followed the same decline.

During the almost 70 years covered by this book, Lionel went from successfully producing expensive electric trains for well-to-do customers to mass-producing lowest-cost-possible toys in a fight for its life. The models reflected Lionel's decisions concerning what would sell and mirrored real life on America's railroads. Collectors informally designate large Standard Gauge trains manufactured from 1923 to 1942 as Lionel's classic models. Any O-gauge, OO-gauge, O27, or HO-gauge trains need not apply. While this narrow distinction is fine for establishing collectors' rules and regulations, for this book, it's more than a bit restrictive.

For instance, during this designated "classic" period, Lionel produced the magnificent Standard Gauge 408E dual-motored locomotive modeled on the S-motor electrics that hauled trains in and around

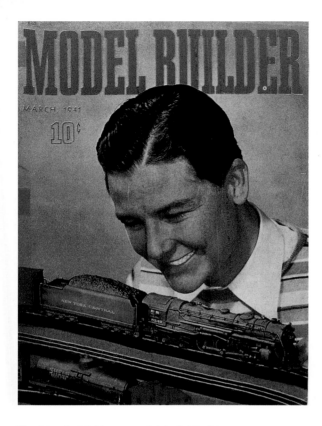

The March 1941 cover of *Model Builder* magazine shows an OO-gauge Hudson on a three-rail track passing a clean-cut lad.

New York City. It's a beautiful brute pressed into service to handle the huge, interior-detailed State passenger cars when the equally beautiful, but less powerful, 381E didn't measure up. Watching the 408 rumble past, towing a string of long, illuminated passenger cars is a real toy train moment.

Conversely, in 1957, Lionel produced an O-gauge train of pastel-colored freight cars pulled by a pink locomotive. The Lady Lionel was designed to appeal to girls, but the targeted female customers stayed away in droves and the Lady Lionel was a sales stinker. Today, the original models are highly prized collectibles and the "Girl's Train" was even reproduced as a flash from the past to run on today's tracks.

From 1948 to 1950, Lionel produced models of the Santa Fe F3 diesel, the long-lived Berkshire steam engine, the GG1 electric, and the Electro-Motive NW2 yard switcher.

Consider the Model 224 steam engine, which, in 1945, had the distinction of being the first locomotive to haul a post–World War II Lionel train. The list goes on. The Pennsylvania Railroad built only one S2 monster steam-turbine locomotive, and it failed. The Model 671 Lionel version introduced in 1946, on the other hand, was hugely popular, spawning a variety of face-lifts and remotorings until the present day. The O-gauge "armored train" of 1917 had no prototype, but a lot of kids helped fight The Great War with this lethal-looking little toy. And if

A circa-1950s Lionel ad trumpets Magne-traction.

anyone doesn't consider the 700E scale-model Hudson of 1937—and even some of its lesser relatives—classic, then we have a problem here. By now, you can understand our spin on what constitutes a classic Lionel train. Some arrived at the right time to become sales winners. Others didn't sell particularly well but were too beautiful—or too esoteric—to exclude. Some models came along in time to save the company from bankruptcy, while others almost caused Lionel to be the final fallen flag of toy train nostalgia. ("Hey, do you remember Lionel?")

A few that were very popular mass-production models stayed in the catalog for years after their introduction and were treated to a variety of colors and special features. One or two allowed you to build your own locomotive. There are also models that represent failed experiments, missed opportunities, and grand, but flawed, visions.

To cover nearly 70 years of toy trains and tell a part of the Lionel story in this format, we stayed with motive power for the most part. Classic Lionel rolling stock is almost another book. We cover freight and passenger cars where they add to the story, as with Lionel's first freight cars, the Model 10 series. Then there are the beautiful State and *Blue Comet* passenger cars and even the incongruity of the stamped-tin, articulated *Rail Chief* passenger train streaming behind the meticulously scaled Model 700E Hudson. By necessity, we do dip into cataloged rolling stock for obvious winners such as the 6464 Series boxcars, or the 3400 Series cars that used an electromagnetic track section to snap open their doors.

During the last decade of our era, few decent, let alone "classic," locomotives were built; strange exploding, shooting, soaring, and generally incongruous railcars battled for parents' dollars and to meet kids' demands for outer space and war toys to combat the Commies. Even HO trains were pushed out the door to tempt model hobbyists, but they died in a tangle of poor planning, execution, and marketing.

This is a book written by train lovers for the kind readers who sent us letters and called us from

A magazine ad shows dad and son with a Pennsylvania Railroad steam-turbine locomotive—the Lionel Model 671.

very distant locations to praise and critique our previous books, *The American Toy Train* (MBI Publishing Company, 1999) and *Lionel: America's Favorite Toy Trains*. We hope we do the subject justice once again. Our previous Lionel book put us in touch with Richard Kughn, the man who took over the throttle at Lionel from 1987 to 1996 and restored the company's former glory. He invited us to use the huge, wonderful collection in his Detroit, Michigan, Carail Museum for the bulk of our original photography. Sue Childers, Carail's

Sunday funny papers offered a rich audience of kids and parents. This example is a preholiday ad from 1953.

curator, was gracious, helpful, patient, and fun to work with.

There's something about holding a big Lionel locomotive in your hands, feeling its heft and complexity, that helps you realize what a delicate interaction of systems is required to get that train on down the track. The motor must run forward and backward and not short out while it powers the wheels, no matter what kind of stylish tin, zinc, or plastic is wrapped around its mechanism. The wheel flanges must grip the track just so in order to follow swift tinplate turns, or leisurely Hi-rail curves. It must clatter over intricate switches without derailing. Couplers must hold the train together and the cars must perform for the engineer every time. Lights illuminate, smoke pours forth, bells chime, and horns blare, all powered by electricity pumped into the rails at a child-safe wattage by a carefully engineered transformer. What other toy is so complex, requires so many interactive engineering decisions, and lives in a

four-dimensional world? No wonder model railroading is the fastest-growing hobby in the United States.

Here is our picture-book look at the world of Lionel through its classic trains from the turn of the century to the edge of oblivion, from which Lionel emerged to become, once again, America's favorite toy train.

–Gerry and Janet Souter
Arlington Heights, Illinois

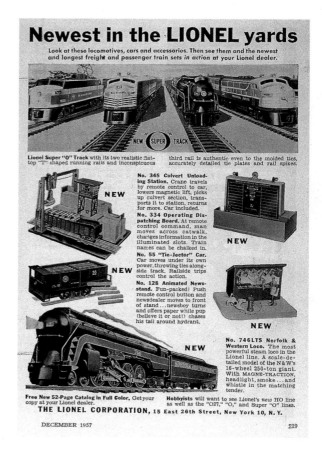

Lionel "Super O" track, action accessories, and the exceptional Model 746 Norfolk & Western locomotive starred in this 1957 ad. The Super O track proved a dud. Magne-traction didn't work with aluminum rails, and the copper center rail sliced into electric pick-up rollers.

13

Chapter 1

Setting the Standard and Elbowing the Competition, 1901–1917

When Joshua Lionel Cohen launched his *Electric Express* cheese-box gondola around its circle of track, he stepped into the unfamiliar world of toy manufacturing. What he designed as an electrically animated bit of toy shop window dressing took on a life of its own: a toy train packaged with track and batteries. Working in his New York City shop at 24 Murray Street with his partner, Harold Grant, Cohen must have looked ahead to his next product, a marketing strategy, and who he would hire if this toy train thing really caught on. But, first, he had to look hard at his competition.

German toy manufacturers Märklin, Bing, and Carette had a lock on snob appeal with their high-ticket wind-up and electric trains and their complete lines of accessories. But two American toy train companies were vulnerable. Ives had an entire line of miniature trains that used clockwork mechanisms to move the locomotives down sectional two-rail tracks, but Edward Ives thought electric trains were a passing fad and that good, solid, cast-iron wind-up locomotives would prevail. After all, they had sold well since the 1860s.

Closer to home, the Carlisle & Finch Company (known as "Manufacturing Electricians") of Cincinnati, Ohio, had marketed a little tin-and-brass trolley car in 1896. It was a huge success, and in 1899 the company added a mining train featuring a tin lump of a locomotive (that was still prototypically correct) and a string of three little dump cars. The whole set cost $5.75, including 18 feet of 2-inch-wide steel-strip track and four dry-cell batteries. The batteries produced 6 volts and cost 25 cents each to replace. A set of four ran the train for an average of 10 hours.

As early as 1910, Lionel brought out electric locomotives modeled on the S-motor engines used in and around New York City, where smokeless hauling was mandated. The Standard Gauge Model 42 shown here came out in 1913 and became a signature piece of Lionel advertising. The 7-pound brute had a single motor when issued, but another was added in 1921 to make it the first dual-powered locomotive in Lionel's fleet.

Conceived as a window display gimmick for Manhattan merchants, the *Electric Express* was Joshua Lionel Cowen's first electric toy locomotive. Produced from 1901 to 1905, it was also Lionel's first success. The gondola later offered link-and-pin couplers to hook up a trailer or two. Its motor is tucked underneath between the four wheels. *Andover Junction Publications via the TCA Toy Train Museum, Strasburg, Pennsylvania*

Five dollars was a week's wages for a working-man, with $10 to $15 considered good pay for white-collar work. So Carlisle & Finch advertised in upscale magazines such as *Scientific American*, while sales agents appealed to the emerging middle class that was discovering disposable income for the first time. It's a good possibility that none of this was wasted on young Cohen.

It appears that for no special reason, except the room needed to stuff the little fan motor into the space between the axles, the *Electric Express* had

flanged wheels requiring a track 2-7/8 inches wide. Meanwhile, Carlisle & Finch had a 2-inch-wide (gauge) track made of almost identical steel strips laid into slotted wood ties. As the new kid on the block, Cohen could have downsized his subsequent products to run on 2-inch track and made money by selling locomotives and rolling stock to Carlisle & Finch owners. But (and this is a big "but" for Cohen) C&F could have done the same, possibly undercutting Cohen's prices or outproducing him. He stuck to his 2-7/8-inch gauge and brought out a

Shown in its natural habitat, on the rug and among the furniture, Lionel's Model 100 Baltimore & Ohio No. 5, unveiled in 1903, tows the Model 800 boxcar (or "jail car," in reference to its barred windows) introduced in 1904. Powered by water-and-acid wet-cell batteries, dry cells, or shunted 110-volt power, both ran on strip-steel two-rail track with rails 2-7/8 inches apart. The boxcar came in powered and unpowered versions.

No. 3. Coal Mining Locomotive and Train.
PRICE, $5.75.

5 to 6 VOLTS.   **¾ AMPERE.**

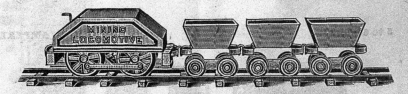

This represents a modern hauling plant as used in our large coal mines. The motor is self-starting, and on top of locomotive is a lever connecting with a reversing switch, by means of which the train may be run backward or forward.

Connection is made from the motor to the wheels by means of double reduction spur gearing with accurately cut teeth. The wheels are spoked, two inches in diameter, and made of iron.

The locomotive is very powerful. It will climb grades and haul the three cars heavily loaded. It will haul 10 to 12 empty cars on a straight, level track. The speed is somewhat less than that of the railways Nos. 1 and 2.

The equipment consists of locomotive, three coal cars, 18 feet of 2 inch gauge strip steel track, and four dry batteries.

Coal cars are iron, **with brass** wheels. They will stand hard usage.

The track may be arranged in any shape. It is better to see that it is level, as the locomotive will run easier and be easier on the battery when track is in this condition. Oil all moving parts of locomotive and train frequently.

Length of train, 18 inches.

Weight, complete, boxed, 13½ pounds.

Coal cars, 25 cents each. By mail, 35 cents.

Track and Ties (strip steel) in 9 ft. lengths, 35 cents. By mail 50 cts.

Extra dry batteries, per cell, 25 cents.

No. 3. Coal Mining Locomotive Only.
PRICE, $3.50.

5 to 6 VOLTS.   **¾ AMPERE.**

This is the locomotive which is used with our No. 3 train. It is sold separately so that customers wishing to add to their equipment can obtain extra locomotives without having to buy the complete No. 3 outfit.

No track or battery is furnished, but the locomotive only.

Length, 7½ inches. Height 3¾ inches. Weight. 2½ lbs. boxed.

—7—

Carlisle & Finch delivered the first American electric toy train set in 1899. The company remained a close rival of Lionel until 1916, when Carlisle & Finch stopped making toy trains.

Lionel also produced Standard Gauge trolleys patterned after actual trolleys plying the streets of New York. This Model No. 1 was offered in 1908.

trolley of his own using his four-wheel motor chassis under a repainted trolley shell produced by the Morton E. Converse Company of Massachusetts.

By 1903, the Lionel Manufacturing Company catalog offered not only the electric trolley but an *Electric Express* made of metal and sporting link-and-pin couplers to attach an unmotored trailer or two. It was Cohen's first train set. More important was the introduction of the Baltimore & Ohio No. 5 locomotive. The model's boxy, double-headed prototype was one of a kind, built to haul freight and passenger cars through Baltimore's extensive tunnel system. Cohen's snappy advertising patter in his catalog included

gems such as, "The armature is laminated and drum wound. To those conversant with electricity the merits of this will be readily appreciated."

By 1904, the B&O loco was teamed up with a crane car, also motorized (a hand crank operated the hook and line), and an unusual motorized boxcar with barred windows and vestibules at each end. Collectors today call it the "jail car." The cars were also offered unmotorized because when all three units were powered up, the batteries, at $1.20 for four, were sucked dry very quickly. Cohen had his railroad, but the game was heating up.

In 1903, Voltamp entered the marketplace with realistic-looking, big electric trains. Additionally,

The "100 Electric Rapid Transit" trolley was issued in 1910 and lasted until 1916. This is the 1915 version. Trolleys were popular models in their day, offering an inexpensive way to start a toy train railroad.

Howard Miniature Lamp Company released its electric steamers, and an outfit named Knapp unveiled its trains in 1905. With competition springing up like mushrooms on a log, Lionel trains needed a push. In 1906, the company got one.

That year, Cohen created a three-rail sectional track that made connecting any kind of configuration easy. Because the center rail always carried the power, tricky reverse loops were no-brainers. Cohen patented the term, "Standard Gauge" for the rails, which were 2-1/8 inches apart. All other track was, by inference, rendered nonstandard.

This marketing coup forced 2- and 1-3/4-inch track (a European gauge used by Electoy in America) to eventually disappear. Standard Gauge became the standard, and the competition had to call its tracks "Wide Gauge" or "No. 1 Gauge." The floodgates opened, and Lionel products chugged and clattered off the drawing boards.

A nifty little 0-4-0 tank-type steam switcher came first in 1906. Curiously labeled the "No. 5," it was followed by its big brother, the beautifully proportioned No. 6, a 4-4-0 steam locomotive with an eight-wheel coal tender. For owners who felt

20

cheated, the No. 5, which carried its own coal and water in a bunker, was given a small tender too.

The No. 6 was also offered in a deluxe version clad in brass and nickel to appeal to indulgent parents with deep pockets. In addition, a series of No. 10 freight cars were offered in 1906, as was a line of passenger cars that appeared in the 1906 catalog but didn't go on the market until the Model 29 passenger car showed up two years later. All of these cars had simple slot-and-hook couplers.

Getting power to the rails was also simplified in 1906 with the introduction of a transformer. The 110-volt electrical power that came into homes was way too hot to run the trains, so the transformer necked the current down to 20 watts using a wrap of iron wire encased in a faux marble box and regulated with a series of brass studs. A swinging lever delivered variations of this power to the track to control speed.

By 1910, Lionel had moved into a four-story factory in New Haven, Connecticut. Cohen had Americanized his last name to "Cowen" and was married to the former Cecelia Liberman. The couple had two children, Lawrence and Isabel. The company's products had grown from the $4 cheese box to a full lineup of locomotives, cars, and accessories. Profits had blossomed to $57,000, and Cowen's big Standard Gauge trains were selling well.

The Standard Gauge trains were marketed to people earning good money and who lived in big homes with room enough for the heavyweight brutes to rumble around the furniture. For the kids who played with what came to be known as the "Rich Boy's Gauge," Lionel came out with the Model 1912, which became the Model 42 a year later. The chunky beast was based on the electric

Lionel's first passenger car came out in several variations between 1908 and 1927. The first was the olive-green No. 3 stamped "No. 29." After 1911, Lionel added the words "New York Central Lines" above the windows. The knobs on the roof represent ventilators.

S-motors that towed freight and passenger cars around the New York Electrified District and replaced smoke- and ash-spewing steamers in the Grand Central Terminal.

Ives had waded in with a line of smaller, more affordable O-gauge trains back in 1910, reaching a wider market. In 1915, Lionel countered with its own O-gauge line of instantly popular S-motor–type electrics that had their own scaled-down freight and passenger cars. Numbering of the line began with the 700 Series; it became the 150 Series in 1917. While the race was primarily with Ives, another upstart was closing in. American Flyer had evolved in 1910 and was selling wind-up cast-iron locomotives out of a Chicago, Illinois, factory run by William Ogden Coleman. They would have to be watched.

While "some damned foolish thing in the Balkans"—the assassination by Serbian nationalists of Archduke Ferdinand and his wife—mobilized the armies of Europe, Cowen moved his 150 employees, mostly loyal Italian immigrants, to a plant in Irvington, New Jersey. They set up shop just in time for the start of World War I. When the beginning of hostilities in 1914 cut off all German imports, American manufacturers leaped into the breech with gusto. This élan was tempered by material and manpower shortages as the United States geared up for what everyone considered inevitable, despite President Woodrow Wilson's protestations for neutrality.

In 1916, 68 toy makers founded the Toy Makers Association of the U.S.A., a trade group "for the betterment of the industry." Guess who was not invited to join this old boys' club.

Since 1905, Lionel's advertising had railed against "unscrupulous manufacturers who have endeavored to duplicate our outfits and sell goods

For more traction power and longer trains, the No. 6, a 4-4-0 American-type locomotive, came out in 1906 and stayed in the line until 1923. Strung behind this example are three Model 10 freight cars, a No. 16 ballast dump car, a No. 15 oil car, and a No. 17 caboose.

Lionel's first steamer was the 1906 No. 5, a 0-4-0 switcher that carried its own coal in a bunker. Later models, such as this 1908 example, had working headlights, eight-wheel tenders, and removable bunkers. It's interesting to note that this locomotive is lettered for the New York Central and Hudson River Railroad, while the tender belongs to the Pennsylvania Railroad.

at lower prices . . ." If a customer wanted an electric train that worked "satisfactorily and for all time," the ads advised, they "MUST GET A LIONEL." Lionel's competitors, who could be counted on one hand, all felt stung by the ads.

In 1917, locked out of the toy train makers' tight little club, Cowen brought out the Model 203 armored locomotive with its two-gun turret and two ammunition cars. He waved the patriotic flag proclaiming, "Play War! Now there's bushels of fun ahead!" In the same catalog, Cowen savaged Ives, though not by name, showing a low-cost Ives passenger car that, compared to the pristine solidity of a Lionel coach, looked like it had made

For the discerning toy train lovers with deep pockets, the No. 6 Special was made to order and made of nickel and brass to boot. It was offered in 1908 and 1909 before becoming the No. 7 and remained in Lionel's product line until 1923.

two or three trips down a cast-iron staircase. The copy proclaimed that the demolition derby victim was "rickety." Lionel's competitors must have wondered where those two armored locomotive cannons were really aimed.

Meanwhile, most of the train manufacturers, Lionel included, cut back on toy making to produce materiel for the war effort. American doughboys slugged it out with the dreaded Huns in Europe until victory in 1918. As the Allies won that war, Cowen enjoyed a victory of his own.

Carlisle & Finch had created beautiful locomotives and passenger cars, but never departed from the handcrafted simplicity of their original designs. After turning a good profit building powerful searchlights for the U.S. Navy and Coast

In 1915, Lionel entered the O-gauge market with a gaggle of small electrics, beginning with the 700 Series that became the 150 Series. This Model 153 is shown with one of Lionel's remarkably sturdy Model 600 passenger cars, which cost 40 cents apiece at the time. Each year the author runs a Model 153 under his Christmas tree, along with three cars that were played with by his father and three uncles 77 years ago.

Guard, the company decided to abandon toy trains and stay with its new product line. C&F's shift into high-powered illumination was an ironic departure, considering the company never produced a working headlight for its toy locomotives.

One of the competitors that pressed Lionel hard in the early days was now gone. Knapp, Howard, Electoy, and Voltamp also lost steam, eventually leaving Lionel and Ives with the lion's share of the market. The situation wouldn't last long, but morale at the New Jersey plant must have been high. The O-gauge market was just heating up and showed great potential for expansion and profit.

By the war's end, the company was known as the Lionel Corporation and was cash rich with $500,000 from military contracts and 500 shares of capital stock worth about $50,000. The company's world was rapidly changing as the Volstead Act passed in 1919, kicking off Prohibition, bootleg booze, speakeasies, and the Jazz Age. Women won the vote, and the ratification process swept across the states. Everyone geared up for postwar prosperity as automobiles putted down paved streets. Warren G. Harding was elected President on his pledge for a "return to normalcy." As wartime tools and dies were stored away, visions of new colorful electrics, spiffy steam locomotives, and inventive rolling stock must have danced in the heads of Lionel's designers and salespeople.

Lionel was perfectly positioned and heading for what would come to be called its "classic period." The people at Lionel had no idea they would create these classics while balancing on a tightrope between sweeping success and crushing bankruptcy.

"Tons of fun now, boys!" Cowen promised with his Model 203 Armored Battle Car, shown here hauling 2 Model 702 ammo boxcars. Touted as a facsimile of real World War I armored trains, it was no such thing. Some thought the guns were actually aimed at Lionel's competition.

Chapter 2

Big Electrics, the Good Life, and the Crash, 1918–1929

With Americans back from the trenches in France, factories reverted to a consumer economy and banks opened for business with new "installment purchase" schemes. And every boy in America, it seemed, wanted a toy train set. In 1918, American Flyer managed to poke an electric motor into its largest O gauge, cast-iron locomotive, but it was still small potatoes. As 1920 closed, Cowen's books were heavy with black ink, to the tune of more than $1 million in sales.

S-motor electric locomotives led the charge, using the ubiquitous Lionel four-wheel motor that continued to evolve and improve. The electric's stamped-tin shell hid all the working parts and was less fussy to manufacture compared to all the bits needed for the steam locomotives. Only one steamer remained in the catalog: the No. 6 4-4-0 with its eight-wheel tender. The tin-shell electrics required only a couple of bells, a pair of headlights, pantographs, some grab irons, couplers, and a spritz of paint before going out the door. They were moneymaking machines.

In Standard Gauge, Lionel's Model 1912 was stripped of some ventilators to become the Model 42. This big locomotive became the flagship of the electric line.

Over in O gauge, the small 150 Series 0-4-0 electrics became bestsellers. The drab color schemes of the 700 and early 150s—dark green, olive green, and light or dark gray—faded away from later 150s and ended with the 200 Series, including the 254 St. Paul–type round-hood locomotives of the mid-1920s. They blossomed into a rainbow of new shades: maroon, Mojave (a sandy brown), wine, brown, and peacock. The 1920s would be a colorful era for Lionel.

Back in New Haven, Connecticut, however, the patriarch Edward Ives had turned some of the reins over to young Harry, who was cut more in

A catalog features the big 408E heavy hauler from Lionel's late-1920s electric locomotive fleet.

29

Shown here is a pair of O-gauge Model 254 electric motors across a trestle. These colorful little locomotives carried on the popularity of the earlier 150 Series and helped bring toy train sets to kids on the lower end of the economic scale. The 200 Series electrics came in a bewildering array of variations.

Cowen's mold. Harry Ives had been peddling the company's No. 1 Gauge (1-3/4 inches between the rails) trains in Europe, but the rebounding German toy industry undercut his prices. He turned his gaze on Lionel's Standard Gauge line and decided to throw Ives' considerable market presence behind a Wide Gauge series of its own, using Lionel's 2-1/8-inch track width.

Cowen looked over the fence, saw Ives' ploy, and in 1921, stuffed a second motor into the Model 42 electric and proceeded to bury Ives with advertising that implied the Ives' single-motor big electrics couldn't haul their own caboose, while Lionel's dual-motored locomotives could practically pull nails out of a wall. Cowen spread the ad campaign in every magazine from *Boy's World* and *Popular Mechanics* to *Colliers* and the Sunday funny papers—just below the fold from "Maggie and Jiggs" and the "Toonerville Trolley".

With the war over, American toy makers expected a banner year, but the grim-faced Germans were at it again. Because of galloping inflation, the value of the deutschmark was dropping faster than banknotes could be printed. The Germans refused to ship toys to American buyers at previously agreed-upon prices. Figuring the Germans were out of the picture for a while, the members of the Toy Makers Association of the U.S.A. raised prices. Buyers, however, afraid they would be stuck with high-ticket goods when prices eventually stabilized, stopped buying from American companies.

Cowen had made a bundle during the war, so he stopped selling and slowed down his manufacturing. While the members of the old boys' club thrashed about, cutting prices to dump inventories, he stockpiled raw materials—brass, tin, and nickel—at bargain bulk prices.

About this time, a bright young Italian lad had worked his way up from soldering tin to the number-two spot at Lionel. Mario Caruso was the enforcer and profit squeezer behind Cowen's jovial *bonhomie*. When Cowen visited the plant floor, everybody had a good laugh with the boss; when Caruso strolled the aisles, everyone who could, hid.

Lionel stuck largely with electric locomotives as its only motive power well into the 1920s. Different sizes were offered in Standard Gauge, the smallest and least expensive of which was the red Model 8 of 1925 to 1932, shown here next to an orange 1928 Model 9U. The smaller electrics added some price diversity to the "Rich Boy's Gauge."

Cowen trusted Caruso implicitly, so when the plant manager visited his relatives in Naples and came back with the wild idea to build Lionel trains over there, the boss listened. They paid Naples a joint whirlwind visit in 1922 and, amid Caruso's wining and dining, the words, "cheap real estate," "cheap labor," and "big profits" did the trick. The Societa Meccanica la Precisa was established under the supervision of Caruso.

The production shift to the sunny Mediterranean eventually had a curious effect on Lionel trains produced there. They began to look like Italian trains, gaily colored and trimmed in silver and bronze with whitewall tires. A profusion of small red, orange, blue, apple-green, and tan electrics were set loose to buzz around miles of Lionel track throughout North America. In 1923, the muscular Model 42 was upgraded to the 402,

MODEL NUMBERS

A word is needed concerning what seems to be a straightforward question of lineage, begets, and begots. It's not that simple for collectors. Lionel was always tinkering with designs. Locomotives might have a round cab, square cab, spoked wheels, solidwheels, brass trim, nickel trim, or no trim. A stripe was added here and a rubber-stamped number there. Still other variations within a design either dinged, whistled, chugged, or blew smoke out the stack.

Model numbers hold the key. For example, a locomotive model number followed by an "E" means it has an electric reverse. But Lionel engineers were not above sneaking a new design wrinkle out the door without telling anyone about it just to see if it would sell. A famous example was Magne-traction (see chapter 4). For the finer points of identification, use any of the Greenberg's guides to Lionel trains or the collector's guide and history books by Tom McComas and James Tuohy.

Also in 1925, Lionel introduced a Standard Gauge St. Paul–type electric, its second-smallest locomotive. The model shown is likely a repaint since no orange Model 10 electrics are listed in Greenberg or McComas and Tuohy references.

Educational toys were in demand throughout the 1920s, and one of the most interesting electrics of the period was the 1928 Model 9U—a kit complete with eight sections of Standard Gauge track. The "U" designation, which stood for "U-Build-It," was also added to the Models 8 and 381 electrics.

Lionel electrics reached their pinnacle in the late 1920s beginning with the 402, a dual-motored heavy-hauler in Standard Gauge that was the go-to locomotive for long trains from 1923 to 1929. As electrics went, it was a plain-Jane model that led to the next step.

tricked out in more brass trim, folding pantographs, and new latch couplers that were intended to allow easier coupling but didn't. The 402 has since been designated by collectors as the first "classic" Lionel locomotive.

As the toy train wars really heated up, backdoor buys and trades also took place. Lionel expanded its offering of accessories—crossing gates, stations, flashing lights, and more—by purchasing them from Ives. Latch couplers were adapted so either Ives or Lionel cars could hook up in the same train.

Just as Cowen relaxed from his dual-motor coup with the Model 402, he peeked over the fence

The 408E started life towing utility trains, but when the mighty 381E couldn't pull the big State passenger cars, the 408E took over. It was the same engine as the 402, but tricked out with more trim, marker lights, and working pantographs. It was Lionel's surprise big winner as the 1920s wound down.

again to see two brothers from Nuremberg looking back. Milton and Julius Forchheimer had arrived from Germany and set up a toy train factory in a three-story building in Newark, New Jersey. Calling their company "Dorfan"—after their two aunts, Dora and Fanny—the Forchheimers had two good ideas: they cut manufacturing costs by

Following Page
A string of Standard Gauge State passenger cars trails a waiting 408E in front of a Lionel passenger station from another era. Each 21-inch passenger car was named after a state and featured full interior details, adding to the drawbar weight. With two motors driving eight big wheels, the 408E had no problem.

casting their locomotives from a copper-zinc compound called "Dorfan alloy," and they offered the locomotives as kits, tailing onto the educational-toy trend sweeping the country. Eventually, Dorfan trains were available in wind-up, "Narrow Gauge" (O gauge), and "Wide Gauge" (Lionel Standard Gauge) lines. Their trains were good, their prices were low, and their pitch to "forward-thinking parents" was seductive.

Cowen first tried kit-built locomotives in 1919, but three years after Dorfan came to town, Lionel reintroduced its line of Bild-a-Locomotive kits, designated with a "U" after the model number for "U-Build It" (9U, 8U, 381U, and so on). As for diecast locomotives, Lionel could do little. Ives-type demolition ads didn't work with Dorfan;

the Forchheimer boys loved to wing their castings against a wall during factory tours to demonstrate their locomotives' durability. Lionel could only hunker down and build better trains.

Ives didn't go away, either. The company introduced an automatic reverse that could be initiated from the transformer instead of a lever atop the locomotive. Even Dorfan offered its Distance Remote Control system.

Shut out by patents, Lionel came up with an electromechanical design in 1926 that changed the locomotive's direction but had no neutral position on the transformer. Any interruption of power on the track could send a high-speed freight or passenger train hurtling backward, accompanied by the smell of a trashing motor. Boxed in by Ives and

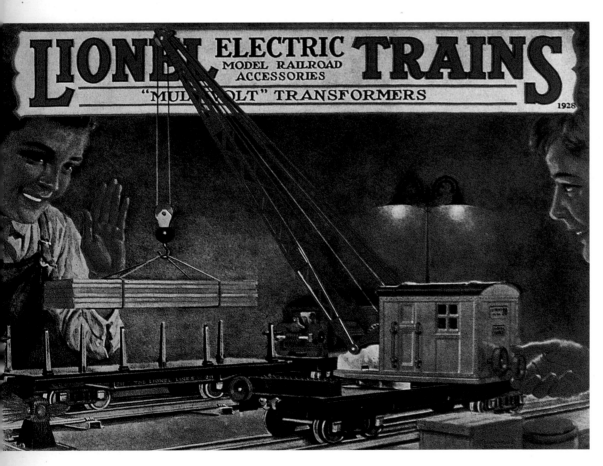

Large operating cars were featured on this 1928 Lionel catalog cover.

Ballyhooed as the ultimate expression in toy train size and design, the 381E of 1928 briefly took center stage until it was discovered the locomotive's single motor couldn't pull the prestige passenger sets. To get the job done, an owner could trade in his or her 381E for a 408E of the same color. The 381E is still the most highly prized Standard Gauge locomotive of Lionel's recognized "classic period."

Dorfan innovations, Cowen soldiered on with trumpet-blasting ads touting Lionel's reverse system as the best in the world.

In 1927, Lionel rolled out the magnificent 408E. The big and beautiful electric traced its lineage to the revered 402, but was much, much more. There was more trim, more dual-engine brawn, and a bigger price tag. The beautiful locomotive trundled off to haul medium-weight passenger sets and other utility work, but its time would come.

Since their introduction in 1910, Lionel's electrics were modeled after the S-motor prototypes familiar to the New York Central and eastern cities.

In 1923, precedent was broken with the introduction of the 380. This "bi-polar" electric featured the fore and aft rounded hoods of the locomotive used by the Milwaukee Road to heave passenger trains over western mountain ranges. It was a neat engine but merely the curtain-raiser for its big brother, the largest locomotive built by Lionel up to that time: the burly 381E.

The 381E premiered in 1928 and in 1929 was teamed with a set of elegant, interior-detailed, 21-inch-long State passenger cars. The 18-inch locomotive, in its olive green, brass-trimmed livery with 12 wheels, looked impressive at the head end of the passenger train. The only problem was the 381E couldn't pull it—a lot of undignified wheel spinning, straining, and grinding sounds came from the 381E's single motor.

From the exile of utility drudge work, the 408E was called up by Lionel to repair the damage. With dual motors humming, it clicked onto the passenger siding, coupled to the heavy train, took up the slack, and rumbled off through the turn-outs into classic toy train history. Lionel's spin doctors immediately offered any disappointed 381 owner a replacement 408E in the same color scheme.

As the 1920s drew to a close, so did one of the great toy train rivalries. Back in 1910, the 29-year-old Cowen had reached a fork in the road: should he continue to compete as a toy maker, or sell out, take his money, and seek other opportunities? He paid a visit to 71-year-old Edward Ives and offered up Lionel on a plate for a price. Ives looked down his nose at the upstart window dresser and refused. In 1928, Ives Company was looking for a way out of its financial hole.

Instead of making money during World War I, Ives lost its shirt on a line of wind-up toy boats. While the craftsmanship was the equal of Lionel and the engineering often superior, the company's financial footing was never solid. By 1928, the only ink used on Ives' books was red. The company's debts dated back to 1926.

At a sad-eyed public sale, Harry Ives watched Cowen and William Ogden Coleman of American Flyer submit a joint bid of $73,250 for the company:

lock, stock, and barrel. For a bargain-basement price, Cowen absorbed his rival. He got hold of the patent on that wonderful reverse system, and he and Coleman split up the tools and dies for the locomotives and cars. American Flyer hung around for a while but eventually bought out of the deal. Lionel used the Ives brand as a low-end outlet until 1932, when the venerable name was consigned to the scrap heap.

Ives' technology came too late for the 1929 catalog featuring Lionel's reemergence into the steam engine world with the Standard Gauge Model 390 locomotive. With gaudy red trim, nickel wheels, and brass piping, this stamped-tin locomotive bore the design eccentricities of the Italian makers. The 2-4-2 wheel arrangement used the ubiquitous four-wheel motor that would, in various incarnations, power Lionel's Standard Gauge fleets until the late 1930s.

In O-gauge, Lionel brought out the 200 Series, a mix of boxy and round-hooded four-wheelers (or St. Paul types) in the variety of colors described earlier. In 1930, the first O-gauge steamers rolled out of the shop: the Model 257 and its twin with a red stripe, the 258. The 257 was compressed in length, toylike, and, like its Standard Gauge cousins, tricked out in gaudy trim.

The expansive 1929 catalog seemed to indicate that Cowen, like the rest of the country, did not foresee the great stock market crash approaching. That year, for $585,000, he purchased a seat on the New York Stock Exchange for his son, Lawrence. When the market collapsed, Cowen lost heavily.

In 1930, when the Bank of the United States failed, Cowen was implicated in a scandal as a result of his brother, Joseph Marcus Cohen's, fast-and-loose money manipulations. Penalties against Cowen came to $850,000 paid over three years. Another $5,000 kept him out of a $6 million lawsuit brought by the state superintendent of banks.

The fate of Lionel was important, not only to Cowen, but to his extended family. Cowen's success translated into the good life for his invested

A 1929 Lionel catalog depicts steam power alongside a big St. Paul–type electric.

relatives and, in particular, his sister, Isabel. She would eventually become a major stockholder and 30 years later introduce Roy Marcus Cohn, Cowen's great-nephew, as the financial savior of Lionel's future. (This was the same Roy Cohn who was Senator Joseph McCarthy's legal assistant during the Communist witch-hunts of the 1950s.) In the 1960s, the younger Cohn would almost accomplish what his great-uncle, Joseph, failed to do in 1930: destroy Lionel completely.

Lionel headed into the Great Depression hemorrhaging red ink and very uncertain about the future. Saving the company would require an infusion of brilliance from Lionel's designers and engineers, as well as a sack full of hard cash to keep the bankers at bay.

Chapter 3

The Depression, Shiny Streamliners, and the Big Hudson, 1930–1942

Besides a humiliating bank scandal, the Great Depression eroding sales, and shelling out a half-million dollars for his kid's seat on the stock market, Cowen in 1930 brought out an inexpensive little train set called the "Winner"—not the "Lionel Winner," mind you, just the "Winner."

Advertised in a separate folder as the "train for Little Brother," the whole set of orange-striped locomotive, cars, track, and transformer sold for $3.25. Cowen hated it almost as much as he hated the wind-up trains he was peddling under the defunct Ives name. In fact, the Winner steam engines were converted from Ives wind-up locomotives. The little trains would bob up again in 1932 and eventually become "Lionel Jr." trains in 1934.

As many customers for Lionel's big, beautiful Standard Gauge trains met their stressed financial obligations by trying to fly off the roofs of their office buildings, no one at Lionel could have foretold what history had in store. Headed by the premier 381E and the 408E electrics, the Standard Gauge mainline motive power was colorful and impressive, while the beautifully built 0-4-0 Model 8 and 9 electrics held down the cheap end of the product line.

Over at the Steam Engine Shop, the Model 260E locomotive represented the largest of the stamped boiler line. Its Vanderbilt tender was diecast to achieve that complex mix of a straight-lined coal or oil bunker and a curved water tank. The 2-4-2 locomotive was also distinguished by its "chugger," a mechanical noisemaker of rotating gears that was supposed to sound more like a locomotive than a cocktail shaker. It didn't.

The Model 264E *Commodore Vanderbilt* O-gauge hybrid also arrived in 1935. Painted solid red, this shrouded steamer hauled a set of three 600 Series red passenger cars to make a train called, appropriately, the *Red Comet*. What made the *Vanderbilt* a hybrid was the use of diecasting for the cab and stamped tin for the streamlined shroud. Later models came out in black, hauling the *Silver Streak*, and in blue, pulling the *Blue Streak* passenger set.

But the hot-ticket engine of this series was the 390E. As with all stamped-tin Lionel steamers Lionel made up until then, the hefty 2-4-2 steamer represented no real-life prototype except by accident. The passenger train it hauled had definite roots, however.

Cowen often rode a four-hour day train operated by the Central Railroad of New Jersey down the Jersey coast. It was called the *Blue Comet* and had blue cars with black roofs. The toy versions of these cars, as visualized by Lionel, practically glowed in the dark. They remain masterpieces of toy train design that rivaled the magnificent State cars that clicked along behind the big 408E electric of the time. The first time these two-tone-blue-with-cream-trim cars saw Lionel track they were towed by a blue 390E. But a new big-dog locomotive waited in the wings. This locomotive was so special it came with a real engineer.

Bob Butterworth drove the New York Central's *20th Century Limited*. He even looked like an engineer in his coveralls, gray-at-the-temples hair, and slightly smudged face. On the cover of the 1931 Lionel catalog, beneath a banner that read, "The Trains that Railroad Men Buy for Their Boys," he stood before a giant pair of drive wheels, showing a brand-new 400E locomotive to his two grandsons, each dressed in white suits with Lord Fauntleroy collars. The caption read, "Just Like Mine."

Of course, the 400E was nothing like Butterworth's big 4-6-4 Hudson. Even in its black paint, the 4-4-4 toy steamer was still trimmed in

Another O-gauge steamer to roll out of the shop in 1930 was the largest stamped-boiler locomotive up to that time: the 260E. By 1933, the much-superior Ives reverse unit was installed in the 260E, along with a "chugger" device intended to reproduce chugging sounds. It sounded more like a martini shaker gone mad.

Having neglected their steam fleet while putting new electrics on the tracks, Lionel in 1929 rolled out a big 2-4-2. The Model 390 was a gaudy winner decked out in copper and brass trim, spoked red wheels, and red-striped running boards. The design reflected their origins at the Societa Meccanica la Precisa factory in Naples.

copper or nickel piping with a red cowcatcher and red-spoke wheels. Behind it was a big Vanderbilt 12-wheel tender. It was a huge, heavy engine that could back into a long string of almost anything Lionel built and walk away without wheel spin. Lionel came out with a two-tone blue version of the 400E and coupled it to the *Blue Comet* passenger set. Once again, Cowen didn't let accuracy get in the way of a good train set, turning the familiar *Blue Comet* day-coach into a long-haul interstate passenger train by adding a sleeper and a dining car.

Over at the O-gauge shops, Lionel builders eventually produced a *Blue Comet* based on the 260 Series locomotive and the 2600 Series passenger cars for the smaller-gauge groundlings. The 263E locomotive was painted two-tone blue and given a snappy 12-wheel Vanderbilt tender adorned with a big Lionel "L" logo.

Bringing out expensive sets as the Great Depression headed toward rock bottom in the early 1930s might have seemed bizarre to Lionel's competitors. In fact, Lionel was slipping toward receivership that had bankers examining every business decision. Lionel had little going for it but its reputation for quality and innovation.

Ives was gone. American Flyer had brought out a premium collection of Wide Gauge trains in 1925 to challenge Lionel and Dorfan, but the big American Flyers were dropped in 1932 as sales plummeted. Dorfan's terrific cast locomotives did well until the famous "Dorfan alloy" began to crack. The passenger cars were made of 17 different parts: a large amount of hand labor that was difficult to sustain as sales dropped and returns mounted. By 1934, Dorfan was through. American Flyer followed in 1936 as Coleman looked for a buyer.

As 1934 rolled around, President Franklin Roosevelt thrashed about to create government relief agencies to stem the country's flow of red ink and save failing businesses. Lionel was in the hole for $296,000 with only about $60,000 and change under the mattress. Again, the toy train market reflected the plight of the railroads. The major rail lines looked for ways to increase revenues while small, undercapitalized railroads succumbed and their unused rolling stock rusted on sidings.

While a feisty mouse was credited with Lionel's salvation, a shot in the arm for both the railroads and toy train manufacturers actually came in the form of two streamliners. "Mickey Mouse saves Lionel" is another myth the newspapers loved, but it was the M-10000 Union Pacific streamliner that did the job.

The Union Pacific Railroad contracted Pullman Car and Manufacturing and the Electro-Motive Division of General Motors to produce a super-lightweight, distillate-powered streamliner called the M-10000. The idea was to make train travel an "event" again—something exciting. Sensing a winner, Lionel pursued the deal and got its hands on the plans. The beautiful yellow-and-brown locomotive with its one-piece articulated train of passenger cars was featured in Lionel's 1934 catalog. The designers decided it was too expensive to produce in Standard Gauge, so the plans were reduced to 1:45 scale and it came out in O gauge. The articulated train wouldn't negotiate sharp O-gauge curves, however, so special O-72 track accompanied the set—all for $19.95. When the sleek prototype raced down the tracks for the first time at 110 miles per hour, it was as big a hit for Union Pacific as the toy version was for Lionel.

As Lionel churned out M-10000 trains, it also built a wind-up handcar featuring the hardworking images of Mickey and Minnie Mouse, licensed from Walt Disney. The car sold for one dollar.

When the Great Depression arrived in 1930, Lionel had absorbed Ives, a longtime rival, and brought out a new steam engine in O gauge, the 2-4-0 Model 257. Lionel maintained the Ives name for some models, and both the Model 257 and its twin, the 258, can be found sporting Ives plaques. As with Lionel's prewar stamped-metal steamers, the stubby locomotives had no prototypes. They looked like what they were—toy trains.

If the rest of the world was plunging into financial despair, Lionel was atop its form. They rolled out the 400E Standard Gauge steamer in 1931 as the big dog of steam haulers. This 4-4-4 monster came out in black and gunmetal with copper piping, brass stanchions, nickel drivers, the usual Italian red trim job, and a Vanderbilt tender. With all the 400E's big-shouldered hugeness, it took a lot of Standard Gauge cars to slow it down.

Engineer Bob Butterfield
of the famous 20th Century Limited *says*

"LIONEL TRAINS

are real...like mine"

"**Y**ES, indeed," says Bob Butterfield, engineer of the famous 20th Century Limited. "They're the only trains I would buy for my boys. No make-believe about Lionel trains. They're real, life-like—just like the good old 20th Century that I drive. The boy who owns a Lionel train is going to learn a lot about railroading. And he is going to have some marvelous fun, too!"

Millions of boys agree with Bob Butterfield. They know that there is no fun in the world equal to operating a Lionel Electric Railroad. Ask Dad to get you a Lionel for Christmas—and send for the FREE Railroad planning book today.

The Lionel Corporation, Dept. A
15-17-19 East 26th Street   New York City

FREE—This Marvelous Lionel Railroad Planning Book

Send us your name and address today and we will send you this beautiful 52-page full color Railroad Planning Book and Catalog absolutely FREE. It tells you all about Lionel Railroads and what famous railroad engineers have to say about them. Write today!

The Lionel Trains and accessories illustrated above may be seen at your local Department Store, Toy, Hardware, Electrical, or Sporting Goods Store. Lionel trains priced from $5.95 upwards.

LIONEL ELECTRIC TRAINS
MODEL RAILROAD ACCESSORIES
MULTIVOLT TRANSFORMERS

Left
Engineer Bob Butterworth is featured in this 1931
American Boy: Youth's Companion magazine ad, along
with the new 400E Standard Gauge steam locomotives.

Lionel emerged from the red. The newspapers put two and two together and Mickey became the hero.

American Flyer, in worse shape than Lionel, made a bid for solvency by grabbing the plans of a streamliner from the Chicago, Burlington & Quincy: the diesel-driven, shot-welded aluminum *Pioneer Zephyr*. The *Zephyr* was also a hit and helped American Flyer's bottom line. Lionel jumped on that wagon too, bringing out a model of the *Flying Yankee*, a twin of the *Zephyr* run by the Maine Central and Boston & Maine railroads. The *Zephyr*-like concept was dumbed-down in smaller, cheaper Lionel sets as well as a key-wind version.

The use of casting à la Dorfan's pioneering concepts allowed the reproduction of the M-10000's streamlined shell. With O-72 track out there for the streamliners, Lionel followed up in 1935 with a stunning gray-and-orange model of

the Milwaukee Road's *Hiawatha* shrouded steam engine. The *Hiawatha* began with an older 4-4-2 Atlantic–style locomotive wheel arrangement, but changed to a more modern and efficient 4-6-2 setup for faster speeds and greater stability. Lionel stayed with the 4-4-2 design, however, and nobody seemed to care.

Also in 1935, Lionel gave some of its locomotives a voice. In 1933, the company had created the "chugger," which turned rods and shook little discs to make a sort of "choo-choo" noise. Not content, some Lionel tenders were fitted with little fans and resonating chambers that produced a realistic, breathy "woo-woo." For the tots, Lionel added a Santa Claus wind-up handcar in 1935, and both Donald Duck and Pluto joined the line in 1936.

With Ives, Dorfan, and American Flyer effectively out of business, Lionel was top dog once again. But for good measure, Cowen took one last look over that fence. What he saw was a former World War I sergeant and toy salesman, Louis Marx, chewing away at the low-end market with tin toy trains that were nowhere near the class of Lionel's offerings—but they were cheap and

In a game of "Can you top this?" Lionel rolled out a beautiful train of two-tone blue passenger cars in 1930, tarted up the 400E in matching colors, and called the whole package the Blue Comet. Built as homage to the great Hudson loco of the New York Central, though not resembling it in the least, the 400E rolled down the track as the flagship of Lionel's Standard Gauge fleet as a vast number of Americans were busy going broke.

Rounding a sweeping curve are models of the Union Pacific M-10000 streamliners, whose prototype both helped restore excitement to American passenger travel and pulled Lionel out of receivership in 1934. The Lionel models were built to 1:45 scale, forming an articulated three-car train. The aluminum version on the outside track is the rarer of the two trains.

cleverly designed. Marx was also connected with department and dime-store chains that thrived on lots of product and fast turnover. Most Marx locomotives were key-wind, but here and there an electric motor found its way under the tin.

Countering this perceived threat, Lionel built a low-end *Zephyr*-type streamliner for kids who played with the Lionel Jr. (kin of the earlier Winner) set. Based on the locomotive Otto Kuhler designed as a copy of the *Rebel* for the Gulf, Mobile & Northern Railroad, it was red and silver and could negotiate the tighter O27-gauge curves. As if to shake his fist at Marx, Cowen even brushed aside his own prejudice

and offered a key-wind version, reversing the paint scheme and adding a battery-powered light.

By the end of 1935, President Roosevelt's grip on the country's economy was stronger. Confidence returned that an end to the economic troubles was in sight. When the last pennies were finally totaled up at Lionel, an actual profit of $154,000 was realized. The company had breathing room to examine its options for the future.

Diecasting was the wave of the future for the toy train industry. Diecasting in zinc alloy, an alloy that didn't crack, was the way to go for modern motive power. (Curiously, Lionel continued to use painted tin for its rolling stock.) Diecasting also allowed the modeling of such complex prototypes as the *Commodore Vanderbilt* locomotive in 1935. This Model 264E represented a crossover that blended a stamped metal shroud with a diecast cab. When rolled out, it came in red, hauling a *Red Comet* set of passenger cars and powered by a red transformer.

The diecast Pennsylvania *Torpedo* shrouded steam engine arrived in 1936. This gunmetal gray, bullet-shaped streamliner was originally issued with narrow T-rail rims, but was later reissued with wider O-gauge flanges for broader market appeal.

Struggling for survival, American Flyer cobbled together a reasonably good-looking 4-6-4 Hudson,

The *Pioneer Zephyr*, unveiled by the Chicago, Burlington & Quincy in 1935, was translated by Lionel the following year into the O-gauge *Flying Yankee*. It stayed in the Lionel lineup until 1941 but remained a novelty, as did its prototype, owned by the Boston & Maine.

With the characters licensed from Walt Disney, the Mickey and Minnie Handcar was created to sell as a $1 novelty. Thousands were cranked out to meet demand. In fact, some press of the day assigned Lionel's financial recovery to the pair of mice. Santa Claus pumped his way out in 1935, followed by Donald Duck and Pluto in 1936. Of the lot, Santa commands the highest price among today's collectors.

even though its four-wheel trailing truck had only two actual wheels and two fake ones. (The Hudson was the darling of steam at that time, hauling such prestigious passenger trains as the *20th Century Limited* from New York City to Chicago.) Cowen did what he always did when competition pushed him and sales needed a shot in the arm: in 1937, he blew the doors off the industry.

At the New York Toy Fair, held each spring for manufacturers to show off their new wares, Lionel displayed a pair of exquisite scale-model Hudsons to be brought out later in the year. The Model

700E 1:48-scale Hudson was made of brass and built by a Swedish firm in New York. Every detail was to exact scale down to the number of rivets. Buyers checked their programs, figuring they had wandered into the wrong booth. Its sister model, the 763, was a plaster casting and towed a Vanderbilt tender. There was somewhat less detail, but it was also half the price of the 700E. Buyers also noticed that the 763 had wide and deep O-gauge wheel flanges and a blind (flangeless) center driver to handle tubular track and tight curves. The brass 700EW Hudson, on the other

The Milwaukee Road *Hiawatha* express steam engine became another Lionel signature locomotive in 1935. The prototype and the model matched until the *Hiawatha* later adopted the 4-6-2 "Pacific" arrangement for increased speed and stability. The Model 250E needed O-72, wide-radius track and came with a set of matching articulated passenger cars behind a 12-wheel tender.

Everyone fell over in 1937 when the scale Hudson 700E locomotive went on sale for $75—it was within three rivets of being an exact model of the famous engine. Its driver rims were narrow for special 72-inch-radius T-rail track, and the tender's coupler was also a scale that coupled to only a few Lionel cars, also brand-new. The loco was built to exactly 1:48 scale. The model shown is easing down an incline made of Super O track, offered in 1957 with a copper center rail, that had thin rails, to accommodate narrow wheel flanges. Today, track built by Gargraves works with the 700E.

hand, had slim-scale flanges like the real Hudsons. To jump from stamped-tin toy locomotives to scale models for a whole different customer demographic was unheard of.

That the 700E was stunning when it came out must have deeply gratified Cowen, who invested between $65,000 and $75,000 to develop the concept and create the dies using a special centrifugal casting process. Special track was also designed for the 700E. "T-rail" featured a 72-inch radius and a flat top to handle the slim scale flanges of the locomotive's driving wheels. (The 700E could run on standard tubular track, but its efficiency was challenged.) The only real problem with the design was pulling power. The 700E's gear ratio was set too low to get off the mark with a long train, though Lionel raised the ratio just before discontinuing the model in 1940.

Priced at $75, the 15-inch 700E was made strictly for the growing hobby market. In 1937, even with the Great Depression winding down, it was a huge sum for a toy train. Then again, hobbyists were accustomed to paying hundreds of dollars for similar quality. In 1938, more adventurous toy train fans could buy the big Hudson as the gray primer 700K kit for $64.50.

For the toy train market, the 224 and 226 diecast steamers were added to the line in 1938. These little engines—the 224, in particular—demonstrated that diecasting could produce considerable detail even in lower-cost models. The 224 lasted until 1941 and then went on to make toy train history four years later.

With streamlining appearing on everything from airplanes to toasters, another sculpted steamer was inevitable. In 1936, Lionel's Model 238 version of the Pennsylvania Railroad K4 shrouded locomotive, nicknamed the *Torpedo*, was rolled out in O-gauge. Lionel's 2-6-2 version displayed how die casting could achieve an accurate rendition of designer Raymond Loewy's complex curves and angles.

Around this time, Lionel fans also enjoyed one other innovation. In 1936, the clumsy latch coupler was dropped in favor of a box-and-hook coupler. This more realistic coupler was upgraded to "automatic" status in 1938 with the help of an electromagnetic track section.

Lionel's entry into the hobby market with the 700E and 763 opened the floodgates for such scale and semiscale locomotives as the model of the Pennsylvania Railroad's B6 switcher.

Numbered 8976 on the cab, the O-gauge Model 701 reproduction of the ubiquitous 0-6-0 prototype was layered with details. When originally offered in 1939, it ran only on the T-rail track created for the 700E. As with the Hudson, the 701 was aimed at hobbyists who relished attention to the prototype, especially for a price lower than they were accustomed to paying for handmade brass models. For the toy train market, Lionel built a Model 227 semiscale engine. Wider flanges were added and the second driver was blind to negotiate tighter O-gauge turns.

As if the 700E Hudson wasn't enough for buyers to chew on, Lionel also introduced a line of OO-gauge locomotives and rolling stock for the scale-model hobby market. These trains were smaller—by more than half—than anything Lionel had built. But, here again, Lionel shot itself in the foot by creating a strictly non-prototype three-rail OO track—an aberration to detail-minded hobbyists.

As new products came off the drawing boards, social changes and national events caused some casualties. The highly profitable Societa Meccanica la Precisa factory in Naples had been nationalized by Benito Mussolini to build weapons. Lionel pulled

Based on the *Rebel* built for the Gulf, Mobile & Northern Railroad, a squeezed-down *Zephyr* of sorts was rolled out in 1936 as the 1700 Diesel for the less expensive O27 and Lionel Jr. markets. The model shown is the 1700D in red-and-silver livery. Plenty of room was allowed between cars so the smaller train could whip around sharp O27 turns.

out and moved all manufacturing back to its stateside plants. This was just in time for the United Paper, Novelty and Toy Maker's Union to finally overcome Cowen's leadership by paternalistic nepotism and set up and unionize Lionel in 1942.

America's economy was still in tatters as the Great Depression wound down. Factories tooled up to be "The Arsenal of Democracy" for Great Britain and her Allies. As the world in 1939 watched German panzer tanks sweep away the Polish horse cavalry, Lionel took one last look at its downward-spiraling sales and pulled the plug on Standard Gauge. The "Rich Boy's Gauge" had run its course.

With diecast steamers, an opening hobby market, and a wide lineup of toy trains for every

Continuing their move toward realistic designs, Lionel's Model 227 0-6-0 steam switcher, based on the Pennsylvania Railroad's ubiquitous B6, was a surprise in 1939. With its realistic slope-back tender, O-scale knuckle couplers, and narrow-flange drivers for T-rail track, it was a stunner. Hand-applied detail abounded, including wire pin lifts for the couplers and grab irons on the boiler. The model shown is a semiscale version with box couplers and a blind center driver for O-gauge track; otherwise it is virtually identical to the scale model.

Toy train manufacturing ceased during the war. Lionel came out with the Paper Train, a cardboard punch-out kit that, when assembled, included a locomotive, three cars, accessories, and 198 inches of cardboard track. *Andover Junction Publications via the TCA Toy Train Museum, Strasburg, Pennsylvania*

pocketbook, Lionel headed into the 1940s with a killer product line. In the officially neutral America of 1939, war in Europe meant financial recovery. But the Japanese messed up those plans by bombing Pearl Harbor. World War II brought virtually all toy making to a screeching halt as American industry retooled to fight the Japanese and the Germans. Lionel hauled out its old World War I navigation instrument plans and tools and went

contract hunting. The only train they manufactured during the war was made of paper.

The Paper Train came in a flat box filled with cardboard punch-out parts that, when fully assembled, gave a tyke a real cardboard train with cardboard track. It was a snore that never paid back the investment. Mostly, kids were content to run the wheels off their prewar sets and wait until the pesky Nazis and Japanese were defeated.

Chapter 4

Lionel's Golden Age of Electric Trains, 1945–1957

With the defeat of Germany and the surrender of Japan in 1945, many American bank accounts were flush with overtime money from war industry work. The G.I. Bill guaranteed a good education to returning soldiers with a desire to make money, make babies, and buy homes with Veterans Administration low-interest loans. After 10 years of the Great Depression followed by four years of rationing for the war effort, Americans demanded new homes, new cars, and new electric trains.

Lionel, American Flyer, and Marx came out of the gate at a full gallop, flush with war contract cash and fistfuls of new designs and innovations. Never were the railroads more in the public eye than during the war. Supplies had streamed across the country to both coasts. Long troop trains had ferried fighting men and women to battle-bound ships and aircraft. Having made the world safe for democracy, America's railroads were ready for a well-earned slice of the fat postwar pie. The toy train manufacturers were ready too.

Louis Marx parlayed friendships with important military men into an overseas inspection tour of German factories, where he established numerous offshore contacts for making trains and toys. Marx was aiming at the low-end, high-volume toy market.

A. C. Gilbert, a hard-driving innovator who made his mark as a toy maker and marketer with the Erector Set in 1913, had bought out American Flyer. He scrapped the company's three-rail O-gauge trains for more realistic

In the banner year 1946, the Model 726 Berkshire was introduced in O-gauge only. The locomotive became the most constantly manufactured engine in Lionel's line, lasting in one form or another until 1968. It offered puffing smoke, a double-worm-gear engine, and a detailed tender with a water scoop underneath. The model shown had Magne-traction added in 1950 and a number change to 736.

61

The unassuming Model 224 locomotive hauled a short freight of prewar tin cars and a prophetic new plastic gondola. Lionel's entry into the 1945 market was inauspicious except for its realistic knuckle couplers. This short train led Lionel toward domination of the toy train market. *Courtesy Andover Junction Publications via the Jim Flynn Collection*

two-rail S-gauge models built to 3/16-inch scale. Using prewar dies to save start-up money and wielding considerable advertising savvy, he went straight for Lionel's market.

Lionel's designers had not been idle during the war. They decided to go for the mass market and forget the hobbyists. The OO-gauge line was discontinued and the scale Hudsons of 1937 were put on the shelf as a noble experiment. Standard Gauge was a memory. The new homes being built were too small for big trains. Besides, the die-cast realism

of O-gauge locomotives eclipsed the popularity of the large tin toys of the "Rich Boy's Gauge." Lionel stayed with a three-rail track but went for more realism in rolling stock and locomotives.

Due to a paper shortage, Lionel was unable to publish a catalog in 1945. Its first postwar products were advertised in a multipage spread in *Liberty* magazine, one big $90,000 ad. A short freight train hauled by the prewar Model 224 steam engine led the line in 1945. The 2-6-2 diecast locomotive was unremarkable and most of its cars were prewar

Decked out in Union Pacific's "armour yellow," the Model 2023 diesel was a hit with O27 operators in 1950. It was also a fair model of the Alco FA. Nobody cared that it was smaller than the O-gauge F3 or had trucks off a switcher—its motor could run all day and its back-to-back A units looked slick swinging through turns. Variations continued until 1969.

models made of stamped tin. Two innovations, however, made the train unique. First, one of the cars, a Pennsylvania Railroad gondola, was made of diecast plastic. This was the shape of things to come. Second, realistic knuckle couplers connected all the cars; these automatic couplers could be zapped open with a special track section and a push-button. Attached to the bottom of each four-wheel truck was a sliding shoe. When the shoe ran over the extra rail in the special track section and a button was pressed, a magnetic coil

Next Page

The S2 steam turbine locomotive design from the Pennsylvania Railroad survived only one prototype, while Lionel's version, the Model 671, launched a series of 20-wheel locos that lasted for decades. This engine arrived in 1946 with hoopla and puffing smoke. Early models used a dimple atop the heated headlamp to catch a smoke pill dropped down the stack. Another version, the 671R, featured electronic control to work couplers, dump coal, and blow the whistle anywhere on the track. It was a great concept that was too expensive.

Continuing the tradition of featuring the latest in electric locomotives, Lionel introduced a model of the Pennsylvania Railroad's GG1 electric in 1947. Though it was a compressed rendition of its sleek, fast prototype, the Model 2332 was realistic. Later versions added dual motors and Magne-traction to haul heavy loads. Power could be routed from overhead wires through working pantographs. The model shown is a 1981 rerelease (Model 8150) with "cat whisker" striping.

behind the coupler was triggered, opening the knuckle. A young engineer could automatically uncouple cars anywhere the special track sections were installed.

American Flyer, meanwhile, was caught flat-footed touting realism as its big selling point. A very unrealistic, albeit smooth-operating, link coupler hooked the trains together. While Gilbert outwardly dismissed Lionel's achievement with the knuckle coupler, link couplers were often airbrushed out of American Flyer catalogs and their designers were put under the lash to build an automatic knuckle coupler that got around Lionel's cast-iron patent.

But Lionel was on a roll. In 1946, the company continued to surprise fans with a small fleet of new locomotives. The first was for youngsters running O27-gauge track across their rugs. Previously neglected with second-rate hand-me-downs from the prestigious O-gauge line, or saddled with tin toys one jump up from key-wind, they finally got their own really hot locomotive.

The Model 221 2-6-4 was a streamlined steamer with a diecast boiler made to look like the Henry Dreyfus–designed J3 Hudsons built for the New York Central's *20th Century Limited* passenger trains. The locomotive was created for operation

In 1949, Lionel introduced a series of semiscale diesel switch engines based on Electro-Motive's NW2. Model 622 was shopped out in 1949 as a test bed for Magne-traction, magnetized axles that afforded a firmer grip on the tinplate rails. The O-gauge Model 623 shown had an improved version of Magne-traction with magnets glued above the axles. The series lasted until 1969 and appeared again in 1970 with a power truck in place of the motor.

on the O27-gauge's lower track and tighter curves. While the 221 could pull only three or four cars without wheel spin, wistful owners of Lionel's low end appreciated the bullet-shaped steam engine.

In 1946, another locomotive also became a signature Lionel product: The Model 671 version of the Pennsylvania Railroad's 6-8-6 S2 steam turbine was massive and looked incredibly busy

churning around the track—and it puffed real smoke. The smoke originally came from a dimpled light bulb—the locomotive's headlight—whose heat dissolved a pellet dropped through the stack. It took a while for Lionel to develop a smoke pellet that didn't (a) kill lab mice, (b) cause the whooping heaves, or (c) induce unconsciousness. They settled on one made of ammonium nitrate that produced

A postwar version of the J3 Hudson was created in 1950 as the Model 773. Designed to run on regular O-gauge track, this locomotive used the same boiler as the scale 700EW with the exception of the smokebox from a 736 Berkshire. The drivewheel spokes were simulated and the pilot truck was reduced in size to navigate O-gauge turns. Because of its one-year run, the model is highly prized by today's collectors.

clouds of nitrous oxide, which was only a greenhouse-effect pollutant. Everyone was happy. O27-gauge owners had their own Model 2020 version of the big steamer. Although, the Pennsy built just one S2, Lionel's versions are still popular more than 50 years later.

The sturdy Model 671 was also issued as the 671R operated by "electronic control." Taking a giant leap forward with technology available at the time, Lionel designers put radio receivers in the turbine's tender and in each of four cars. From a push button console, Little Billy could blow the whistle, uncouple cars, and dump coal anywhere on the track. Unfortunately, the concept not only didn't work well, it cost $200. The set hung around for a year and then was quietly discontinued.

The anchor of the 1946 fleet, however, was the Model 726 2-8-4 Berkshire steam engine. The 726 equaled the longevity of the 671 in Lionel's lifetime locomotive lineup and had the snob appeal of being offered only in O gauge. Loaded with diecast detail, the engine looked good in front of both passenger and freight trains. Under its hood, the Berkshire boasted a double-worm-gear drive that Lionel's marketing folks christened the "Atomic Motor" after the bomb that won the war against Japan.

The double-worm gear actually originated with the Model 671. Prior to that, steam locomotives typically had only one set of drivers that powered the front and rear axles of an eight-wheel driver set; the two center axles were without flanges and barely touched the rails. By 1947, the Atomic Motor would be replaced with a single-worm gear

From 1957 to 1966, Lionel took a shot at the hobby market with a line of HO trains. However, they lost confidence in realism and scale appearance, as they did with the 1937 Hudson and OO scale, lapsing into play-value rolling stock that mimicked their toylike O-gauge offerings. Today, as with this repainted and decaled 1970s Alco GP switcher, some Lionel HO bits and pieces can still be found, however worse for wear. *Courtesy Harry Dode Collection*

that was mounted at a 30-degree angle and powered only the rear driver set. A slug of weight was added over the second and third driver sets to improve traction.

Needing a star product for its 1947 line, Lionel reached back to its original love of electric locomotives. In 1934, the Pennsylvania Railroad's call for a new electric locomotive to replace its clunky P5a led to a concept by famed industrial designer Raymond Loewy. Shopped out as the GG1, 139 of

the sleek, powerful locomotives were built by 1943. They were capable of pulling virtually any load hung on their drawbar, they raced passenger cars along at 100 miles per hour, and they were smoke-free, making them welcome in any terminal with overhead wires.

Lionel recreated the Pennsy GG1 in O-gauge. Though it wasn't a steam engine, the sleek loco became a favorite of Cowen. It slid easily down the track, ran fast, and still looked prototypical. Though

This Model 685 is one of the small Hudsons built by Lionel to fill the "big" steam locomotive gap left by the failure of the full-size 773. The 685 employed a brand-new boiler designed for the Santa Fe version of this all-purpose hauler. In the next decades, the small Lionel Hudsons proliferated like mushrooms on a log. The model shown is crowned with an Elesco feedwater heater above the smokebox, giving it a beetle-browed, muscular look.

In 1956, Lionel returned to its electric loco roots, introducing the 2350 Model of the General Electric EP5. In orange, white, and black New Haven Railroad livery, Lionel's model was accurate except for the four-wheel truck usually used on the F3 diesel. The O-gauge locomotive also shared the F3 motor and borrowed its pantographs from the GG1. The EP5 used a plastic shell, so insulators were not needed when power was routed from overhead wire rather than the tracks. The model lasted until 1960.

a bit crushed in length to negotiate tinplate curves, its Brunswick green, five-gold-stripe, Loewy-designed livery was accurate. Eventually, a second motor was added to increase pulling power. The GG1 would be called back several times over the years to shore up the product line.

If the GG1 was a winner in 1947, the products of 1948 were atomic in their effect on the company. Wartime records proved the operating efficiency of the big F1 and F3 diesels from General Motors' Electro-Motive Division, and the postwar railroad scene moved into diesel power. Cowen hated diesels. They looked like bricks lumbering down the tracks—no busy valve gears churned away, no smoke—nothing. But marketing reality overruled his prejudice.

Kids out West had no models of the real trains they were accustomed to seeing. All Lionel products were based on eastern designs and liveries. Cowen approved a short 10,000-unit run based on an F3 painted in the Atchison, Topeka & Santa Fe's red-silver-and-yellow "war bonnet" colors. But this was allowed only if a New York Central version was also released *and* the Santa Fe and New York Central railroads helped pay for the expensive dies. A few million F3s later, Cowen had to admit he was wrong. The Santa Fe version went on to become the single most recognized Lionel product.

Due to the cost of Lionel trains, a lot of kids in postwar America could only watch the company's big diesels motor around department store windows. If they wanted an electric train, their parents had to buy from Louis Marx. Marx toys and

This Model 627 is dressed in Lehigh Valley livery with one-axle Magne-traction. Lionel's O27 Model of the GE "44-tonner" diesel switcher, the 627, was huge in proportion to its prototype and had neither light nor horn.

trains were clever, colorful, and cheap. In 1952, the company even managed to turn out a Santa Fe diesel with five cars, track, and a transformer for half the price of Lionel's. Marx's low-end tin-smithing chafed Cowen. He didn't want just the middle and top ends of the toy train market: he wanted *all* of the market.

The Scout series of unimposing 2-4-2 steamers for O27 track answered the need for a cheap loco-motive. The prewar Model 1684 was the series' direct ancestor, held over and modified after the war to haul short freights as part of starter sets—some as cheap as $25 or less. In various iterations, the series hung around and sold well for years.

A diesel switcher was the big news in 1949. Lionel's Model 622 was designed to resemble Electro-Motive's NW2. The 1,200-horsepower prototype was used as a utility-yard goat on railroads across the country. What made Lionel's version different from all the other locomotives the company had ever built was Magne-traction. Lionel magnetized the locomotive's axles for a better grip on sharp tinplate curves and improved pulling power. The 1949 version's magnetism quickly dissipated, however, which supported Lionel's wise decision to not mention Magne-traction in catalog copy until it was perfected.

Maddeningly, just as Lionel was ironing the bugs out of Magne-traction in 1950, the Korean War was kindled and all aluminum-nickel-cobalt (alnico) magnets were diverted to the armed forces. Lionel was forced to pull the feature in 1951.

If the loss of magnets was a bother, Lionel was in good company. The railroads, too, realized their slice of the postwar pie had dwindled to a sliver. New airlines swiped passengers, and interstate trucking siphoned off freight business dramatically. A noose of draconian federal regulations that did not apply to planes or trucks quietly throttled America's railroads.

In 1950, Lionel chose to revive the big Hudson of 1937, or at least a kissing cousin of the formidable 700E locomotive. The Model 773 was introduced with a train of heavyweight passenger cars as the Anniversary Set commemorating Lionel's 50 years in business. Close inspection of the 4-6-4 Hudson revealed the same boiler as the original 700E. The smoke box, however, came from the 726 Berkshire and the pilot wheels were made smaller so the big engine could yank around tinplate O-gauge curves. Today, collectors prize this locomotive. It is rare because, back in 1950, it failed to stir the blood of Lionel fans and was scrapped by 1951.

If the big ideas in 1950—Magne-traction, which dissipated too quickly, and big, dumbed-down steamers—were a bit of a bust, the bottom line was shored up by the Model 2023. Bargain-basement tads (including your author, who gamely played with their O27 Scout trains while secretly envying the stylish, muscular O-gauge locomotives) were stunned and amazed. Now they had their own diesel streamline.

Painted in Union Pacific's "armour yellow", the 2023 was a model of Alco's FA. Granted, the 2023 was smaller than the O-gauge F3, its trucks were the same design as those on Lionel's 622 NW2 switcher, and the prototype FA blew so much smoke it was dubbed an "unofficial" steam engine. But nobody cared. The popular Model 2023 stayed in the lineup with several paint schemes until the dark days of the late 1960s.

With the Korean War escalating, Lionel returned to war materiel contracts. Toy train manufacturing continued through the Korean War years, however, and by 1953 Lionel achieved peak earnings of $32.9 million. Two-thirds of the toy trains sold in America were Lionels and ran on 25,000 miles of three-rail track.

Unveiled that year, the Model 685, complete with smoke, Magne-traction, and a whistle, was typical of a class of "small" Hudsons. It came just after the Anniversary Set debacle. An earlier small Hudson, the Model 2046 introduced in 1950 and brought back in 1953, used the boiler off a 726 Berkshire. Designed for both O gauge and O27, small Hudsons featured blind middle drivers and tiny pilot trucks. Like the Santa Fe F3 diesel, the 685 was a western locomotive that gave kids who lived where the sun shines all the time a locomotive they recognized. Lionel's real coup with the 685 was ease of assembly, making it less expensive to build.

Lionel once boasted that it had saved the mom-and-pop hardware store by creating Lionel dealerships. With the population shifting to the suburbs, the distribution game changed. Large malls surrounded by even larger parking lots were anchored by huge discount chain stores that brought fast-turnover merchandise to the new peripatetic suburbanites. A new struggle developed over shelf space. As hot new toys moved in, traditional toys were crowded out. Expensive train sets were pushed aside by Barbie, G.I. Joe, Robby the Robot, and jet fighters by Revell and Monogram. Palms became sweaty in the Lionel design shop.

6464 BOXCARS

Often trailing behind Lionel locomotives were long strings of the ubiquitous 6464 Series boxcars. Introduced in 1953, these well-proportioned boxcars began with the 6464-1 Western Pacific "Rides Like a Feather" car and eventually proliferated into several hundred variations! Eventually, the 11-inch 6464 body was mated to a mechanical frame. When the car passed over an electromagnetic track section, the boxcar door was zapped open at the push of a button. When the door popped open, a little rubber man looked out. Soon he was tossing out boxes or sacks, or even sweeping with a broom, adding animation to the normally static cars.

Lionel had previously issued animated rolling stock, beginning with the 3462 Milk Car issued in 1947. In 1949, three more 3400 animated boxcars were introduced on the series' 9-inch frames. Curiously, when Lionel began to animate the 6464 boxcars, they reverted to 3400 Series numbers. Such action cars and accessories became more important as the weapons of the Cold War between the United States and the Soviet Union spread to toy store shelves in the mid-1950s. The romance of the railroads was winding down compared to that of exotic rockets, jet planes, and talking robots. A train could no longer just roll down the track; it had to do something: unload, load, light up, fire a rocket, or explode. At the same time, another coup was taking place on store shelves.

Sharing the popularity of the 6464 boxcars was Lionel's operating 3400 Series that used the electromagnetic track section to uncouple cars. When a pull-down plunger in the frame was zapped by the magnet, the door flew open and a little rubber man peeked out. The variety of on-the-fly operating cars added excitement and play value to the rolling stock because they did not have to be parked to go into action. This Western Pacific Model 3474 was offered in 1952 and 1953.

Lionel had to design and market newer, more colorful trains, so the company fell back on its success with the garish diesels. The Fairbanks-Morse Train Master diesel locomotive used a single 2,400-horsepower engine formerly used to power submarines. The hulking locomotive was designed as a heavy-duty hauler for long freight and coal drags in hill country. Because of its radical design, railroads did not jump at the chance to own one. Only 127 were sold. Conversely, Lionel's Model 2321, a 17-inch block of gray plastic shell over simulated six-wheel trucks, was instantly popular when introduced in 1954. Its Lackawanna gray-and-maroon paint scheme was hardly eye-catching, but the locomotive's twin vertical motors and Magne-traction made it a brawny loco designed to haul long trains, just like its prototype. That series and the GP7 and GP9 diesels that followed beginning in 1955 would eventually offer buyers a rainbow of railroad liveries.

Doggedly, Lionel did cling to a few quality introductions. First offered in 1956, the Model 2350 New Haven EP5 rectifier joined the GG1 (and borrowed its pantographs) to expand Lionel's electric fleet. The locomotive on which it was modeled was designed to rectify AC current from overhead wires into DC current to power the motors that drove the wheels. Lionel's version of this gaudy orange-black-and-white double-ender locomotive riding on tracks borrowed from the F3 diesel was later expanded to other road names. Its finish was never perfected on the plastic shell, and today EP5s with most of their decals intact are highly prized.

Another switch engine was added to Lionel's yard operations fleet in 1956. This model copied a prototype that was designed to get around a union rule that determined a one- or two-man operation by the size of the engine. The General Electric "44-tonner" was a center-cab switcher operated by one man. As originally offered, only one axle had Magne-traction.

The year 1957 was the watershed in Lionel's attempt to maintain its share of the toy train market. As far as the competition was concerned, American Flyer was in the worst shape, having

Rumbling along in all its pink glory, the Lady Lionel set of 1957 was a tragic attempt to reach the female market. For $50 you could embarrass your daughter or niece with this pink loco, buttercup-yellow boxcar, frosting-pink gondola, lilac hopper, robin's egg–blue boxcar, and sky-blue caboose with light. Oddly enough, these same colors are used, without a second thought, on today's prototype grain hoppers. The 2037 came with all the goodies: smoke, Magne-traction, and marker lights—and it ran well. The set hung around through 1958.

overpromised and underdelivered on new models. As American Flyer saw sales slip, the company sought non-railroad lines such as race cars and chemistry sets. Only Marx thrived, with designers blowing 250 toys out the door each year, calling back what didn't sell, repainting it, and sending it out the door again. Louis Marx had wisely proven he could supply everything from yo-yos to talking airplanes, exactly meeting the needs of the new fast-turnover merchandisers.

Lionel pursued a number of attacks. First, it reapproached hobbyists with a line of HO trains in

1957, producing excellent trains with the Italian firm Rivarossi. When the alliance broke down, the American manufacturer Athearn took over. Quality suffered, but it was toylike "play value" design decisions that sunk the line. The costly experiment failed and, by 1966, hobbyists had abandoned Lionel in droves. During the 1970s, HO would be resuscitated in Lionel's Mount Clemens, Michigan plant run by General Mills' Fundimensions. It would go nowhere.

Another tack was novelty marketing. Lionel brought out a pastel-colored train set for girls. The

Lady Lionel, with its sky blue, pink, and buttercup yellow color scheme rivaled only the Ford Edsel as a marketing stinker. The train was reissued for collectors in the 1990s, and original models are highly valued. In 1957, however, they gathered spiders' nests on dealer shelves.

The truly sublime locomotive of 1957, and one generally accepted as one of Lionel's most elegant designs, was the Model 746 Norfolk & Western shrouded steam engine. The 4-8-4 beauty was a model of the N&W J-class prototype considered one of the most perfectly designed steamers ever built. It was efficient, fast, and rugged.

Another innovation was "Super O" track, an attempt at a more realistic three-rail design. Durable, molded-plastic ties supported a more prototypical T-rail rather than tubular tinplate. The almost invisible center rail was razor thin and made of copper. Unfortunately, finicky track connectors were easily lost, aluminum rails nullified Magnetraction, and the copper center rail scored grooves in the electrical pickup rollers of locomotives and rolling stock.

As the Soviet Union's *Sputnik* satellite beeped above their heads, many Americans felt they were in a race for survival in an unstable nuclear age. The railroads continued to struggle for survival and toy trains slipped from birthday and Christmas lists. As 1957 ended, Lionel's fortunes were on the edge of a long, steep nosedive.

Lionel's postwar push reached its apogee with the Model 746 Norfolk & Western. This streamlined 4-8-4 engine is, arguably, the most elegant steam locomotive Lionel ever offered in O-gauge. With the exception of smaller running gear borrowed from the Berkshire, the 746 strongly resembles its prototype Norfolk and Western J-type, a legendary multipurpose locomotive. The model shown has a "short stripe" 1958–1960 tender. Today, only the 1937 Hudson outranks the 746 as a desirable collectible.

Chapter 5

Will the Last One Out Please Turn Off the Lights? 1959–1969

If Lionel management and employees in 1959 could have seen 40 years into the future, the agony and angst of the next 10 years might have been easier to bear. As it was, Lionel's design and marketing staffs cast about wildly, trying to keep their trains on the shelves. Their dealership base dwindled as chains chewed up hardware stores, and department stores succumbed to discount chains. Television spread across the country like a rash, bringing outer space, rockets, robots, fast cars, and jet planes into homes along with seductive toy commercials tied to children's programming. Both American Flyer and Lionel made valiant attempts at creating television programs and placed their trains in morning shows, late-night shows, and even primetime and dramas, but saw no visible success at the bottom line.

Worse still, the great driving force behind Lionel's success, Joshua Lionel Cowen, lost confidence in his company and withdrew from its activities. His son, Lawrence, never really a train guy, was ineffective as boss. Family members who had staked their financial futures on Lionel stock panicked. After personally attending a board meeting and listening to the company's plans for the coming year, Cowen went home and sold his stock to his great-nephew, Roy Marcus Cohn.

This was the same Roy Cohn who had insinuated himself into the public eye as attorney for the hearings chaired by Wisconsin junior Senator Joseph McCarthy. With his career stoked by appearances at McCarthy's elbow during the infamous Communist witch hunt of 1953 and 1954, Cohn established a legal practice in New York. By the time he headed up the investment group that acquired Lionel in 1959, Cohn had earned a

The heart-tugging disintegration of the great Lionel lineup of the late 1940s and early 1950s is brought home by comparing the Model 2023 Union Pacific Alco FA—the darling of the O27 crowd back in 1950—with the Model 202 UP Alco FA seven years later. The latter featured a dummy coupler, single-axle Magne-traction, and a headlight. A virtually featureless collection of FAs paraded through the 1960s.

The year 1959 saw Lionel fighting for shelf space with robots and rockets. With the sudden popularity of westerns on TV, Lionel designers cobbled together a model of a 4-4-0 American-type, diamond-stack, wood-burning locomotive dubbed the Model 1862 *General*. The Five Star General set originally consisted of a flatcar with six horses, a vestibule baggage car, and a matching passenger coach with a whistle. The loco came in Super O and O27. The later Model 1972 *General* locomotive received smoke and Magne-traction.

reputation as a clever, rapacious, fast-dealing money manipulator and entrepreneur. Lionel's product line from 1959 to 1969 managed to stave off submersion until Lionel's rescue by General Mills in 1970, but it was a close call.

The 1959 catalog would be the last real train catalog from Lionel for years to come. In it, the product line managed to simultaneously move back in history and forward into a frightening and uncertain future. As a new locomotive offering, Lionel chose a prototype from the Civil War, a diamond-stack, wood-burning 4-4-0 locomotive called the *General*. Westerns were big on television and a Disney film entitled *The Great*

Locomotive Chase had featured the namesake engine as part of a true story of Civil War heroism. The *General*, issued in Super O—that realistic-looking track with more ties and a wider, 72-inch radius—was a decent locomotive decked out in gaudy red cab and wheels, a cowcatcher, and brass trim around the steam and sand domes. The engine reminded some collectors of Lionel's Italian Period in the 1930s, when all its steam locomotives were similarly decorated.

The *General* offered Magne-traction, three-position reverse, a working headlight, and smoke. Trailing behind the *General* was a wood-stacked tender, a horse car, and both an illuminated baggage and chair car; all five pieces were sold together as the Five Star General set.

Over the five years the *General* was in Lionel's lineup, it varied from realistic, as with the Five Star General set mentioned, to fantasy cars that began a trend toward the outlandish action cars that persist today. One example featured a sheriff and a hobo chasing each other around a gondola full of crates. When the TV western craze went away, so did the *General*.

Another fad that took hold in the United States during the 1950s and 1960s was the stirring,

patriotic need to defeat the godless Communists. Nuclear tests popped off regularly, atomizing atolls in the Pacific and rattling dishware in Nevada. The Soviets hurled men, women, and dogs into space with regularity. If they could do *that*, surely they could hurl a barrage of intercontinental ballistic missiles down on the United States.

In a scramble to meet this threat, the American space program turned rocket after rocket into scrap as the novel projectiles detonated on or just above their launch pads. Cities across the country installed Nike missile facilities to gun down plunging Soviet ICBMs

One of the cars added to the *General* was the Model 3444 "cop and hobo" animated gondola created in 1957 and hooked up to the O27 *General* in 1959. The car features a cop chasing a hobo, animated by a hidden strip of 16-millimeter film stock to which the figures are attached. The car was revived in 1980 as the Model 9307. Rolling stock couldn't just sit there any more—it had to *do* something.

The Model 614 Alaska Railroad O27 diesel switcher served two purposes. First, it was a spin on the NW2 and, second, it celebrated Alaska's admission as a state *and* an "outpost of freedom." No NW2 ever had a dynamic brake doodad and no dynamic brake ever looked like the yellow carapace attached to the 614. The model appeared in 1959 and lasted through 1960.

that crossed the Distant Early Warning line in northern Canada. Kids learned to identify Soviet MiG jet fighter and Bison bomber silhouettes. Lionel's bid to arm the youth of America with lethal toys started slowly but built up steam.

In 1959, Lionel issued the *Alaska* version of the venerable Model 622 switcher that surreptitiously introduced Magne-traction back in 1949. The Model 614 bore little resemblance to the fairly accurate 622. The *Alaska* was a low-end offering with a headlight and nonoperating couplers. It was also a throwback to the days before electronic "distant control" reverse: a lever atop the hood was flicked to send the locomotive off in the opposite direction. Changing direction in tunnels or under bridges was not an option.

The 614 was painted blue with a "dynamic brake" unit cast in canary-yellow plastic affixed in front of the operator's cab. Advertising copy surrounding the *Alaska* pointed to its namesake's admission into statehood in 1959. Lionel also pushed the Cold War envelope by noting that the new state was the farthest frontier of the United

The U.S. Army Mobile Missile Launcher was a motorized unit shopped out in 1959 to blast four missiles at whatever enemy was available and tow any of the military and space action cars Lionel designers frantically cobbled together. Coupled to the launcher is a Model 6650 IRBM (intermediate range ballistic missile) launch flatcar that was also offered in olive drab as part of a military set.

To douse the flaming, post-apocalyptic rubble, Lionel created firefighting apparatus. Waiting at the station, a motorized 1958 Model 52 Fire Car is parked next to a 1959 Model 3512 Ladder Company Car. Both are equipped with nozzle-wielding firefighters in rotating chairs. A rubber belt rotates a light shield and the little man on the ladder car, while a rack-and-pinion device moves the firefighter on the fire car. The fire car uses a bumper at either end to change direction. Both units lasted until 1961.

Lionel's multiuse, four-wheel-power truck became a mainstay of a fleet that could dart around a layout like busy bees. This Model 56 Minneapolis & St. Louis Mine Transport car represents Lionel's minimalist approach to motive power in 1958.

States and boldly faced the Communist threat across a narrow neck of water.

An armada of Army, Navy, Marine Corps, and NASA cars and motive power rolled from Lionel's arsenal. From 1959 to 1964, the passive, utilitarian locomotive and its train of goods were transformed into weapons of war. This period of toy train mayhem was marked by a series of cars that fired missiles, blasted cannons, and launched rockets. To make sure there was adequate ammunition, Lionel designers provided flatcars stacked with additional missiles and rocket fuel. A submarine provided

reconnaissance and located the elusive enemy, especially if he was lurking in the bathtub.

Less lethal but no less improbable were cars hauling *Mercury* capsules, radar scanners, and cars that launched balloon targets. To mop up after the bloodbath, there were firefighting apparatus and a really dangerous-looking Radioactive Waste car that carried away the slag with its lights flashing.

In competing with other toys of mass destruction, Lionel offered targets too. An ammo dump exploded by means of a mousetrap device when a missile landed on it. Target cars flew apart when

A motorized unit using a power truck could also be more sophisticated, as with this Model 53 Rio Grande snowplow that added leading and trailing wheels to become a 2-4-2. On the later Great Northern Model 58 version, the snowplow rotated.

struck by rockets, and a complete missile range was available to keep Little Billy's eye sharp and reflexes honed.

A number of powered units ran on four-wheel-power trucks under a variety of molded plastic shells. These trucks powered a track-cleaning car, snow blower, track-maintenance cars, and a fire truck that changed direction whenever it hit a barrier.

Hauling around this motley collection of rolling stock was an equally motley choice of motive power. A small Hudson was the top end of the line, while other small steam engines that were sold with simple loop-of-track starter sets popped up with a variety of number changes.

Magne-traction was replaced with rubber "gripper" tires on the drive wheels. Zinc castings were replaced with plastic shells and plastic

trucks, and couplers were pinned to the tenders and other rolling stock. The crowning beauty of the steam engine line, the Norfolk & Western 746, was unceremoniously dumped in 1960. In 1966, even the big-shouldered Berkshire steamer was scrapped; inventory sell-offs billed as "special order engines" carried the model into 1968 and then it was gone.

Two locomotives, the Model 246 and descendants of the once-loved 2023 Alco FA, best represent this slide in quality. For two Quaker Oats box tops and $11.95, a buyer could own the plastic Model 246, four cars, a transformer, and enough track for an oval. The 246 was just one of a number of 2-4-2 engines shopped out at the cheapest cost to haul plastic-molded freight cars. No smoke unit, a reverse lever on top of the boiler,

The Model 246 2-4-2 steam engine represents the nadir of Lionel's steam fleet in the early 1960s. It had a plastic boiler, plastic motor, plastic tender with plastic trucks—in this case a Model 244T slope-back tender—and plastic couplers. For two cereal box tops and $12, it could be bought in a plastic three-car set with a plastic 35-watt transformer.

and one driving rod on each side of the engine were its minimalist features. Some of Lionel's steam engines were even being built in Japan.

The Alco FA–based locomotives fell on bad times with the painted-plastic 200 Series. Among them was the Model 202, a sad echo of the stalwart 2023, that first O27 diesel streamliner. The Model 202 presaged the move toward cheap train sets

designed to move off discount-store shelves. It achieved that goal.

These low-end locomotives often had no coupler in front of the A unit, while the coupler in the back was a plastic dummy. The locomotives variously offered no light, no horn, and no Magne-traction. They were also cheap to produce, held together in many cases by a single screw. Basically, they were

Actually a dolled-up 246, the Model 249 added an orange stripe and real motor. The sad fleet of 2-4-2 locomotives and their plastic rolling stock were a lose-lose product for Lionel; nobody wanted steam engines—especially not *cheap-looking* steam engines.

Model 2023s stripped down for the marketplace. They proved to be popular with the discount chains, because their low price—about $15 for a loco and a small train of cars—helped move them off the shelves. Lionel had sales winners that steadily eroded their reputation.

Though Lionel was in crash-and-burn mode, there were a few bright spots. Their rolling stock was often charming. The Model 6445 Fort Knox Gold Reserve car was a 6464-type boxcar with two large windows in each side revealing stacked piles of gold bars, hardly a secure way to transport a nation's bankroll. Another car that still gets a laugh is the Operating Giraffe Car: a giraffe's head poking through the car's roof is counterbalanced to slide down out of harm's way when it hits a "tell-tale"

Though the company was in chaos in the early 1960s, Lionel designers managed to keep a sense of humor while cleaning out their desks. This is a later version of the 6445 Fort Knox Gold Reserve car, showing off our nation's wealth through two large windows of a 6400 Series mold originally made for an aquarium car that revealed swimming fish.

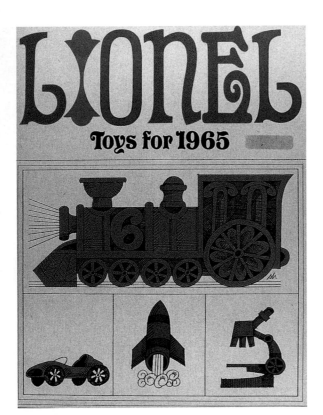

By 1965, trains were only part of Lionel's product line. The market wanted rockets, fast cars, and robots. Anything on rails was no longer relevant.

device that warns of low tunnel and bridge entrances. But the car that most symbolized the 1960s was the 3434 Poultry Dispatch Car. Triggered by an electro-magnetic track section, a little rubber man sweeps out the chicken droppings.

In late summer 1965, the air was heavy with sadness and unease in Lionel boardrooms. On September 8, Joshua Lionel Cowen died of a stroke. He lived long enough to see his hard-built empire fall into ruin. A. C. Gilbert of American Flyer had died in 1961, and what was left of that company was snapped up by Lionel in 1967 and added to its ossified inventory. Lawrence Cowen, Joshua's son, died in 1968. Only Louis Marx was left to continue the pursuit of the next great toy.

On May 6, 1963, Roy Cohn ducked out the back door of a shareholder's meeting at New York City's Essex Hotel, just two jumps ahead of a deputy sheriff trying to have the CEO's limousine towed

The Model 3376 Operating Giraffe Car was issued from 1960 through 1966 and reissued in 1969. It featured a giraffe that ducked its head when it brushed under a "telltale" that indicated a bridge or tunnel ahead. A counterbalanced cam underneath pushes the head back up when the obstruction was well astern.

away as payment against a debt. Cohn's stock went to a group of tinkering entrepreneurs who successfully buried Lionel's train business under a collection of race cars, chemistry sets, and radios while they hacked away at the tangle of companies accumulated by Cohn. There was no Lionel catalog in 1967.

By 1969, the company's name was attached to a string of Lionel Leisure stores that began to see red in their books. Lionel trains, along with their tools, dies, spare parts, and tracks, were relegated to warehouses. Faithful employees and designers who had stayed until the last were cut loose.

EPILOGUE

It was quite a ride. Between 1900 and 1969, the company that Joshua Lionel Cowen built picked its way through the modern history of the twentieth century and managed to survive. Even if the only remaining Lionel asset that had any value in 1969 was the magical name itself, the heartbeat was still there. The Lionel name was enough to attract a new type of entrepreneurial force that grew through the 1970s—the corporate conglomerate.

Large corporations sought to expand product lines by accumulating other companies. Cereal manufacturers chose toy companies to stay close to their kid marketplace. General Mills scooped up a number of names and assets—Rainbow Crafts, Regal Toy, Kenner, and Parker Brothers—and leased the Lionel name for a royalty consideration. These toy builders were placed under General Mills' imposed dollar and sales quotas.

For Lionel, General Mills was the great savior, rescuing the train line from the scrap heap. All those tools and dies waited for the resurrection. General Mills infused capital into the name and many former employees were called back to rebuild the toy train line.

As crates were opened and new administrators tried to find their offices, two key factors would impact the resurrection. First, in the real world, railroads were sliding toward ruin. In 1970, the Rail Passenger Act created the National Railroad Passenger Corporation and the Amtrak (American Travel and Track) logo. All rail passenger service was placed under the government umbrella, but with no guarantee of survival. This federally mandated passenger service was bleeding away any profits made from the already reduced freight traffic. Freight orders, meanwhile, continued to slug it out with the trucking industry.

With the degradation of train service went the romance of the railroads that had fueled the success of toy trains. Diesel locomotive drivers and diesel truck drivers wore the same clothes. Many kids had never even seen a steam engine in motion. Trains were mostly responsible for tying up traffic at grade crossings.

For starters, Lionel, operating out of General Mills' Fundimensions Division, had to jump-start the children's market. The second key factor was even more important: the growth of the adult hobby market into toy trains.

Recalling the Lionels and American Flyers of their youth, a large number of hobbyists were building toy train layouts and collecting everything from the former glory days. These people were finicky about quality and accuracy and they had deep pockets for the models that caught their fancy. They could also doom a model that failed to live up to their standards. Every new product from Lionel was subject to a win-or-lose throw of the dice as it ran the gauntlet between collecting hobbyists and finicky rivet-counters. Kids were being elbowed out of the market.

As 1970 began and Lionel moved forward once again, this time with the Grain Grinders at the throttle, the days ahead were uncertain. But at least the trains were rolling, and Joshua Lionel Cowen's company once again had a future down the track.

With a man in the doorway busily sweeping out chicken droppings, the Model 3434 Poultry Dispatch boxcar created in 1959 delighted little tykes until 1966. No more fitting symbol could be found for the state of Lionel. What was left of their trains ended up in warehouses either as auction fodder or sale assets. As moms outfitted their toddlers with Lionel Leisure Wear, out there among the cereal kings, resurrection was at hand.

TECHNICAL RESOURCES

Greenberg, Bruce C. *Greenberg's Price Guide to Lionel Trains, 1945–1983*. Edited by Roland LaVoie. Sykesville, MD: Greenberg Publishing Company. 1983

Greenberg's Guide to Lionel Trains, Vol. I: 1901–1942. Edited by Christian F. Rohlfing. Sykesville, MD: Greenberg Publishing Company. 1988.

Greenberg's Guide to Lionel Trains, Vol. I: 1945–1969. Edited by Paul V. Ambrose, Alan Stewart, and Joe Algozzini. Sykesville, MD: Greenberg Publishing Company. 1996.

Greenberg's Guide to Lionel Trains, Vol. II: 1901–1942. Edited by Christian F. Rohlfing. Sykesville, MD: Greenberg Publishing Company. 1988.

McComas, Tom, and James Tuohy. *Lionel: A Collector's Guide and History, Vol. I: Prewar O Gauge*. Radnor, PA: Chilton Book Company. 1993.

McComas, Tom, and James Tuohy. *Lionel: A Collector's Guide and History, Vol. II: Postwar*. Radnor, PA: Chilton Book Company. 1993.

McComas, Tom, and James Tuohy. *Lionel: A Collector's Guide and History, Vol. III: Standard Gauge*. Radnor, PA: Chilton Book Company. 1993.

INDEX

Lionel America's Favorite Toy Trains
ISBN: 0-7603-0505-6

The American Toy Train
ISBN: 0-7603-0620-6

Vintage Disel Locomotives
ISBN: 0-7603-0507-2

Narrow Gauge Steam Locomotives
ISBN: 0-7603-0543-9

Super Steam Locomotives
ISBN: 0-7603-0757-1

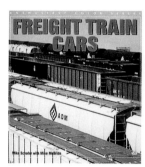

Freight Train Cars
ISBN: 0-7603-0612-5

Locomotive
ISBN: 0-7603-0996-5

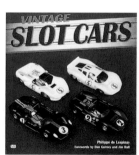

Hot Wheels Cars
ISBN: 0-7603-0839-X

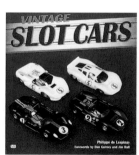

Vintage Slot Cars
ISBN: 0-7603-0566-8